Roald Dahl's
Matilda
THE MUSICAL

MUSIC & LYRICS BY TIM MINCHIN

ISBN: 978-1-78038-777-2

Visit Hal Leonard Online at
www.halleonard.com

Roald Dahl's
Matilda
THE MUSICAL

BOOK
Dennis Kelly

MUSIC & LYRICS
Tim Minchin

ASSOCIATE CHOREOGRAPHER
Ellen Kane

ASSOCIATE DIRECTOR
Luke Sheppard

ASSOCIATE DIRECTOR
Lotte Wakeham

COMMISSIONING DRAMATURG
Jeanie O'Hare

CASTING
David Grindrod CDG
Hannah Miller CDG

CHILDREN'S CASTING
Jessica Ronane CDG

MUSICAL DIRECTOR
Alan Berry

EXECUTIVE PRODUCER
André Ptaszynski

EXECUTIVE PRODUCER
Denise Wood

ORCHESTRATION & ADDITIONAL MUSIC
Christopher Nightingale

SOUND DESIGN
Simon Baker

LIGHTING DESIGN
Hugh Vanstone

ILLUSION
Paul Kieve

SET & COSTUME DESIGN
Rob Howell

CHOREOGRAPHY
Peter Darling

DIRECTOR
Matthew Warchus

Roald Dahl's Matilda

THE MUSICAL

MUSIC & LYRICS BY TIM MINCHIN

Photographs of the original London cast at the Cambridge Theatre
by Manuel Harlan. © Royal Shakespeare Company.
Cover image artwork and design by aka.

First performance at The Courtyard Theatre,
Stratford-upon-Avon, 9 November 2010

First performance at The Cambridge Theatre,
London, 25 October 2011

First performance at The Shubert Theatre,
New York, 4 March 2013

First performance at Sydney Lyric Theatre,
Australia, 28 July 2015

With thanks to Tim Minchin, Chris Nightingale,
Caroline Chignell and Kevin Wright.

Foreword

Creating, Discarding, Collaborating

In mid-2009, in between a comedy tour and the birth of my son, I spent six fun-but-fretful weeks writing songs for Dennis Kelly's wonderful (but tuneless!) stage adaptation of Roald Dahl's Matilda. I got about ten tunes written – many of which survived and are in this book.

But the job was far, far from over.

'The School Song' lacked menace, 'Loud' lacked intent, 'Telly' lacked brevity, and Trunchbull's tune lacked sports equipment. The character of Hortensia was deemed too dominant for our version of the story, so she had to go, along with her epic tribute to antagonists, 'Now That She's Gone', and her battle cry, 'Revolting Children'. (Happily, the latter was later revived.)

But worst of all, we suspected that Matilda's song, 'Magical', was not gutsy enough for her (it wasn't!) and Miss Honey's 'Not Enough Days' was too saccharine for her (it was!)... and suddenly our two protagonists had no songs at all!

What with loads of performing and babies and what-have-you, it took me almost a year before I was able – with the help of Dennis and director Matthew Warchus – to figure out what these complex, subtle, slightly broken characters would sing. 'Naughty', 'Quiet', and 'My House' were not completed until just before our final workshop. Some songs come easily and some need to be painfully extracted. Both ways are fine!

Without the hard work, brilliance and positivity of Dennis, Matthew and the folk at the RSC, these songs obviously wouldn't exist at all. And without the wonderful Chris Nightingale, they would just be a series of harmonically related bits, rather than parts of a cohesive piece. I am so grateful to everyone in the *Matilda* team.

And I am hugely grateful to the Dahl family for trusting all of us with one of the great works of the greatest children's writer of our time.

One more acknowledgement: Casey Bennetto's 'The ABC of Love' was the source of the trick in 'The School Song'. I rang him and asked if I could use the idea, and he didn't hesitate. Casey's irrepressible love for music, theatre and creativity is hugely inspiring to all who know him.

I hope you enjoy playing and singing these songs four ninths as much as I enjoyed writing them.

A Brief Tip For Chord-Heads

Because I'm not a sight-reader, chords are the basis of my musical world.
As a result, I wanted this book to really work for people who read 'lead-sheets'
as well as those clever monkeys who read dots. To that end, here's a bit of a tip
for intermediate pianists (sorry – guitarists will have to fend for themselves!).

A lot of what I wrote for
Matilda was built around
this particular chord shape.
Check it.

Those with a bit of jazz knowledge will probably
recognise the shape as the third inversion of the
dominant 13th chord. In this case, you stick an F in
the bass and create an F13, with the right hand thus
expressing the 7th, 9th, 3rd and 13th of the chord.
Sweet.

But it's a wonderfully versatile shape!
Leave the right hand there, but replace
the bass note with a B, and it becomes
a B7($\sharp$5 $\sharp$9)... also sometimes expressed
as B7(alt). Funky.

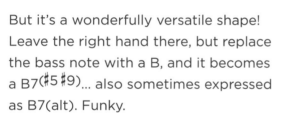

With a C bass, it's a Cm$^{6/9}$. With an A bass, it implies an Am$^{11(\flat5)}$.
With a B$\flat$ bass, I suppose you get a B$\flat$maj^{13}. And so on.

But perhaps most importantly for you Matilda
players, if you simply play the above shape over
an E$\flat$ bass, it becomes a very simple expression
of an E$\flat$maj$^{7\sharp11}$. Take note, because maj$^{7\sharp11}$
chords are all over the place in this book!!

And that's it from me. Go! Play! Sing!

TM
Nov. 2012

Miracle

Words & Music by Tim Minchin

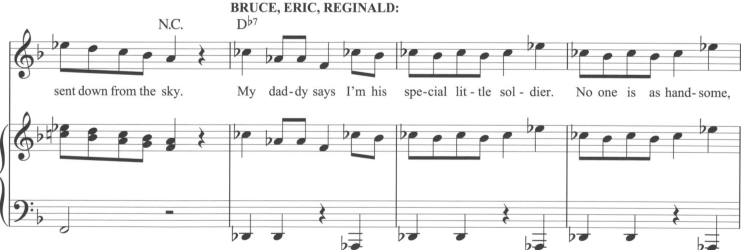

BRUCE:

strong as me. It's true he in-dul-ges my ten-den-cy to bulge, but I'm his lit-tle sol-dier, hup two four free!

AMANDA, HORTENSIA:

My mum-my says I'm a mi-ra-cle, one look at my face and it's plain to see. Ev-er since the

day doc chopped the um-bi-li-cal cord, it's been clear___ there's no peer___ for a

NIGEL, TOMMY:

mi-ra-cle like me. My dad-dy says I'm his spe-cial lit-tle sol-dier,

no one is as bold or tough as me. Has my dad-dy told ya, one day when I'm old - er,

I can be a sol - dier and shoot you in the face!

TEACHER:

One can hard-ly move___ for beau-ty and bril - liance these days.___ It

seems that there are mil-lions of these one - in - a-mil - lions these days.___

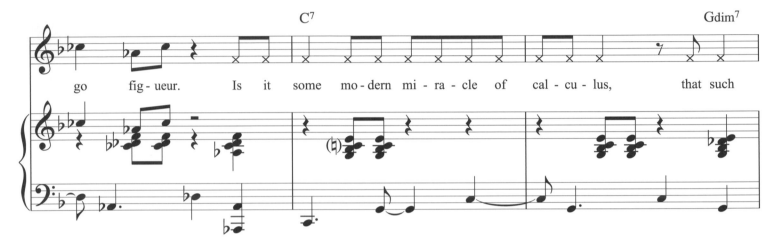

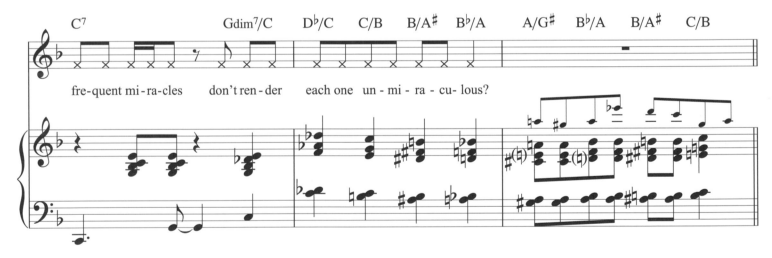

ALL KIDS:

day doc chopped the um - bi - li - cal cord, it's been clear_ there's no peer_ for a mi - ra - cle like me!

LAVENDER:

My mum - my says I'm a pre - cious bar - re - li - na. She has nev - er seen a pret - ti - er bar - re - li - na.

MUM 2 AND DAD 2:

She says if I'm keen, I have to cut down on the cream. But I'm a bar - re - li - na, so GIVE ME MORE CAKE! Take an - oth - er

MUM 2:

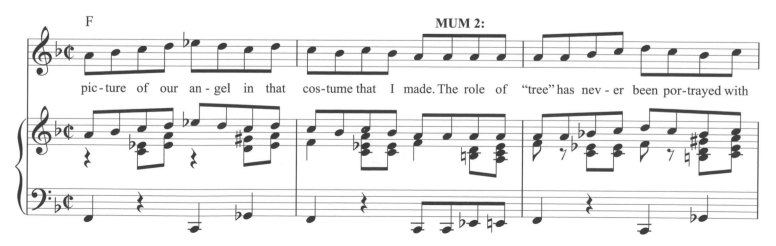

pic - ture of our an - gel in that cos - tume that I made. The role of "tree" has nev - er been por - trayed with

20

norm? I know to voice it's fright-ful form.

(Take an-oth-er...)

CHILDREN:

My mum-my says I'm a mi-ra-cle one look at my face and it's plain to see. Ev-er since the

day doc chopped the um-bi-li-cal cord, it's been clear__ there's no peer__ for a

mi-ra-cle like me! My mum-my says I'm a mi-ra-cle, that I'm as

ti - ny and as shi - ny as a mir - ror ball. You can be all cy - ni - cal, but

it's a truth em - pi - ri - cal. There's nev - er been a mi - ra - cle, a mi - ra - cle as mi - ra - cle as

molto rall. ♩ = *c.* **100**
DOCTOR:

me! Ev - 'ry life___ I bring in - to this world re-stores my faith in hu - man kind.

Each new-born life,___ a can - vas___ yet un - paint - ed. This still un - bro - ken

22

DOCTOR AND COMPANY:

skin, this un-cor-rup-ted mind. Ev-er-y___ life is un-be-lie-va-bly___ un-

-like-ly. The chan-ces of ex-is-tence al-most in-fi-nite-ly small.___ The most

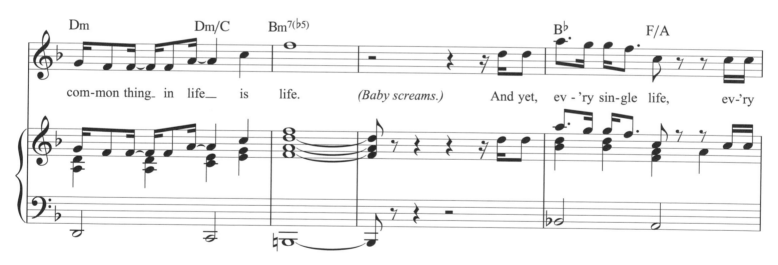

com-mon thing___ in life___ is life. *(Baby screams.)* And yet, ev-'ry sin-gle life, ev-'ry

new life___ is a mi-ra-cle!___ Mi-ra-cle!___

In 4, quite freely

MRS WORMWOOD:

Oh,_____ my un-der-car-riage does-n't feel quite nor-mal. My
skin looks just re-volt-ing in this foul fluo-res-cent light. And this gown is noth-ing like the se-mi-
-for-mal, se-mi-Spa-nish gown I should be wear-ing in the se-mi-fi-nals_ to-night. I should be
danc - ing the Ta-ran-tel - la. Qui mon

fel - la I-ta-li-a-no. Not dressed in

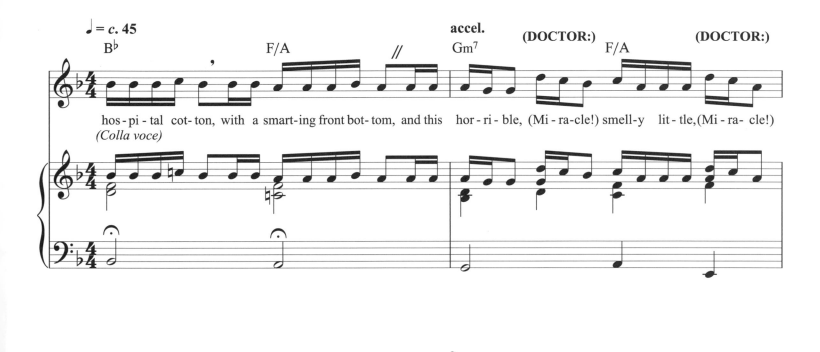

(Colla voce)

hos-pi-tal cot-ton, with a smart-ing front bot-tom, and this hor-ri-ble, (Mi-ra-cle!) smell-y lit-tle,(Mi-ra-cle!)

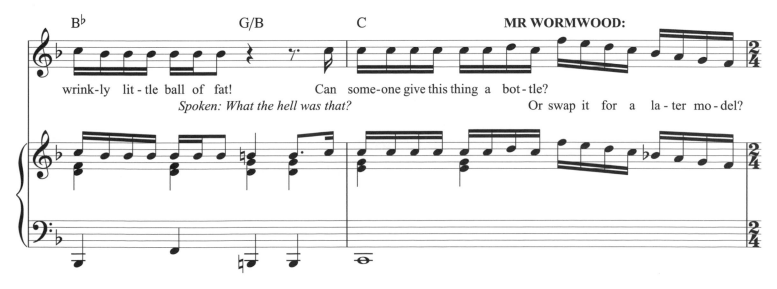

wrink-ly lit-tle ball of fat! Can some-one give this thing a bot-tle?
Spoken: What the hell was that? Or swap it for a la-ter mo-del?

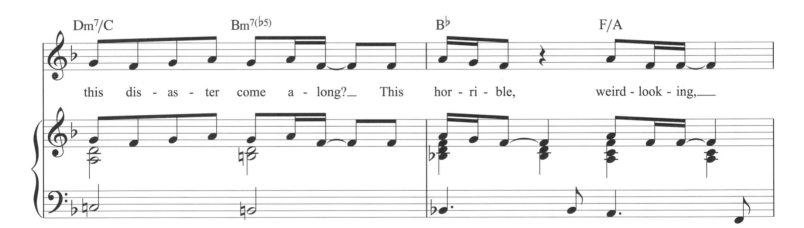

MR WORMWOOD:

mi-ra-cle! Ev-'ry life's a mi-ra-cle. Most beau-ti-ful mi-ra-cle I have ev-er seen! I can't

PRIEST AND PARENTS:

find his frank and beans! Ev-er-y___ life is un-be-liev-a-bly___ un-like-ly. The chan-ces of ex-

-is-tence al-most in-fi-nite-ly small._____ The most com-mon thing_ in life_ is

life. And yet, ev-'ry sin-gle life, ev-'ry new life_____ is a
(Hup two four free!)

27

mi-ra-cle!＿ Mi-ra-cle!＿ Mi-ra-cle!＿

KIDS:

My mum-my says I'm a mi-ra-cle, one look at my face and it's plain to see. Ev-er since the

day doc chopped the um - bi - li - cal cord, it's been clear＿there's no peer＿ for a mi-ra-cle like me.

KIDS:

My mum-my says I'm a mi-ra-cle, that I'm as

ADULTS:

My mum-my says I'm a

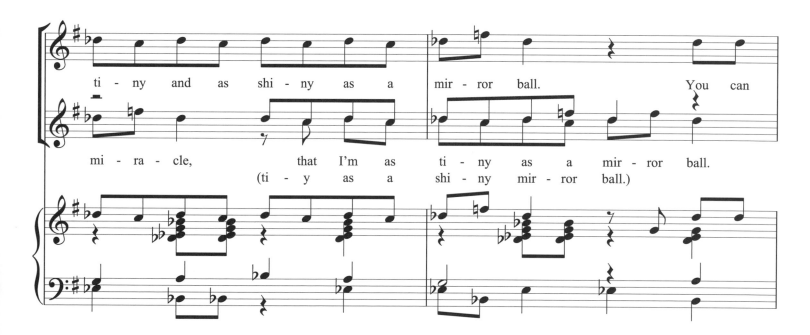

ti-ny and as shi-ny as a mir-ror ball. You can

mi-ra-cle, that I'm as ti-ny as a mir-ror ball.

(ti-y as a shi-ny mir-ror ball.)

be all cy-ni-cal, but it's a truth em-pi-ri-cal. There's

You can be all cy-ni-cal, but

29

nev - er been a mi - ra - cle, a mi - ra - cle as mi - ra - cle as me!

it's a truth em - pi - ri - cal. This mi - ra - cle as mi - ra - cle as me!

Meno mosso
MATILDA:

My mum-my says I'm a lou - sy lit - tle worm. My dad - dy says I'm a bore.

My mum-my says I'm a jumped-up lit - tle germ, that kids like me should be a-gainst the law.

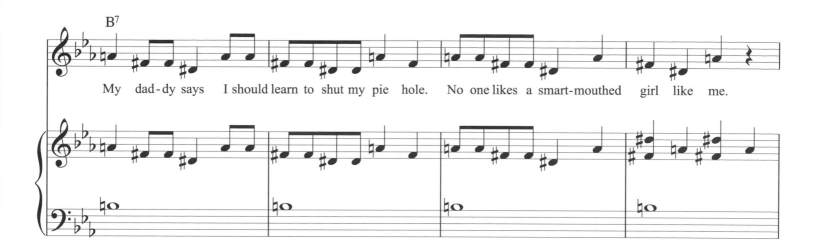

My dad-dy says I should learn to shut my pie hole. No one likes a smart-mouthed girl like me.

Mum says I'm a good case for po-pu-la-tion con-trol. Dad says I should watch more

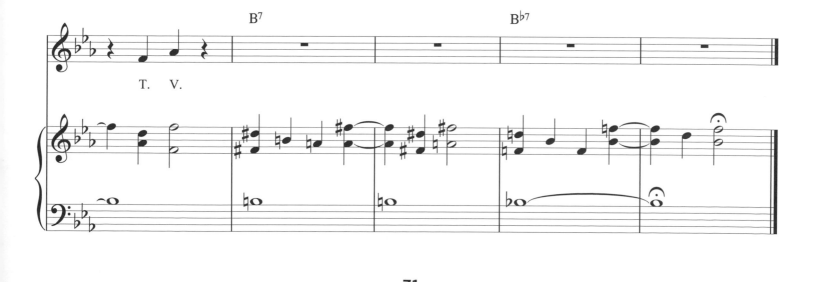

T. V.

Naughty

Words & Music by Tim Minchin

Ro - me - o and Ju - li - et: 'twas writ-ten in the stars be-fore they e - ven met that

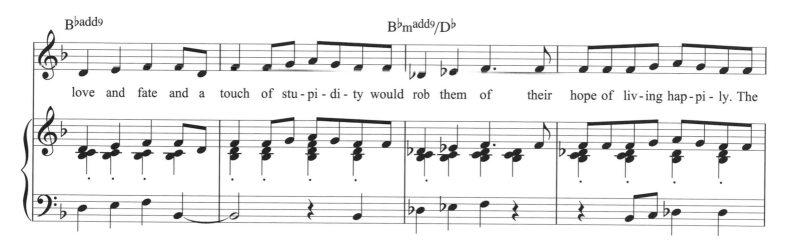

love and fate and a touch of stu - pi - di - ty would rob them of their hope of liv-ing hap-pi - ly. The

end-ings are of-ten a lit - tle bit go - ry. *(Finger snaps)* I won-der why they did-n't just

change their sto - ry. We're told we have to do what we're told, but sure - ly

some-times you have to be a   lit-tle bit naugh - ty.

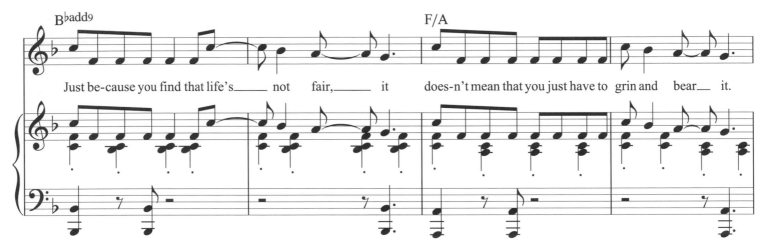

Just be-cause you find that life's___ not   fair,___ it   does-n't mean that you just have to grin and   bear___ it.

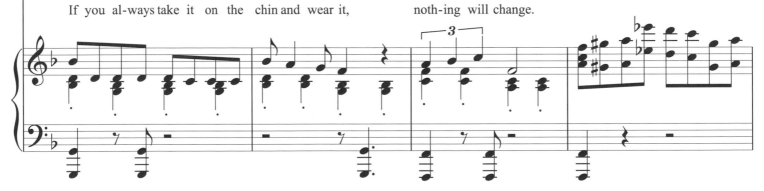

If you al-ways take it on the   chin and wear it,   noth-ing will change.

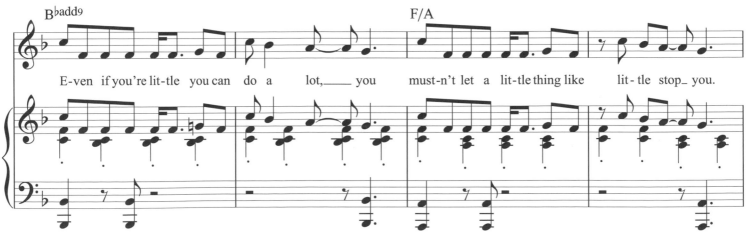

E-ven if you're lit-tle you can   do a   lot,___ you   must-n't let a lit-tle thing like   lit - tle stop_ you.

Gm / C⁶ / A⁷/C♯ / N.C.

If you sit a-round__ and let them get on top,__ you might as well be say-ing you think that it's o-kay, and

A / A/C♯ / Dm / C / B♭maj7 / N.C. / B♭ / C/E / F / B♭/C

that's not right!!

Fadd9 / C

Cin-de-rel-la, in the cel-lar, did-n't have to do much as far as I could tell. Her

B♭add9 / B♭madd9

God-moth-er was two-thirds fair-y, sud-den-ly her lot was a lot less sca-ry. But

what if you have-n't got a fair-y to fix it? Some-times you have to make a lit-tle bit of mis-

- chief!

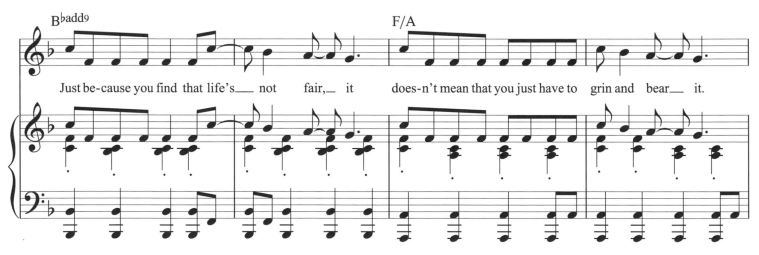

Just be-cause you find that life's___ not fair,___ it does-n't mean that you just have to grin and bear___ it.

If you al-ways take it on the chin and wear it, noth-ing will change.

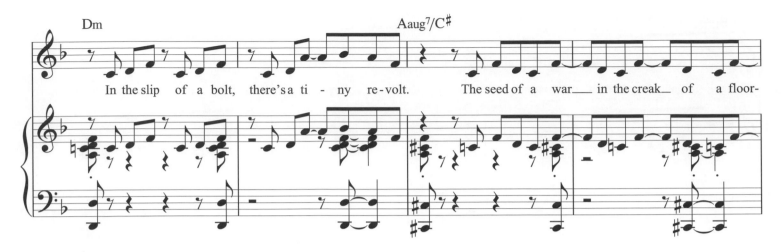

In the slip of a bolt, there's a ti - ny re - volt. The seed of a war__ in the creak__ of a floor-

- board. A storm can be - gin with the flap of a wing. The ti - ni - est mite__ packs the might - i - est

sting. Ev - 'ry day starts with the tick__ of a clock.__ All es - capes start with the click__ of a lock.__

__ If you're stuck in your sto - ry and want to get out,__ you don't have to cry,__ you don't have to shout!

'Cause if you're lit- tle, you can do a lot,__ you must - n't let a lit-tle thing like lit - tle stop__ you.

If you sit a-round and let them get on top,__ you won't change a thing.

Just be-cause you find that life's not fair, it does-n't mean that you just have to grin and bear__ it.

If you al - ways take it on the chin and wear it, you might as well be say - ing you

think that it's o - kay. And that's not right. And if it's not

right, you have to put it right. But

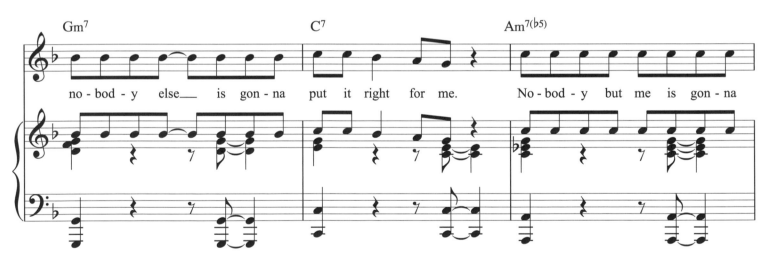

no - bod - y else___ is gon - na put it right for me. No - bod - y but me is gon - na

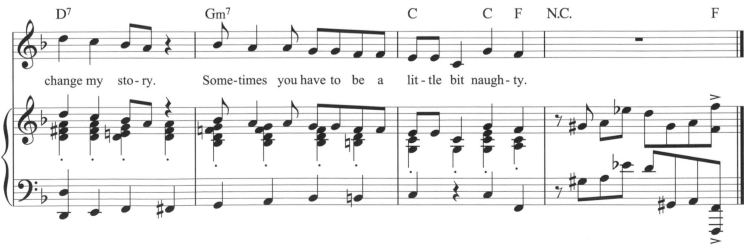

change my sto - ry. Some - times you have to be a lit - tle bit naugh - ty.

School Song

Words & Music by Tim Minchin

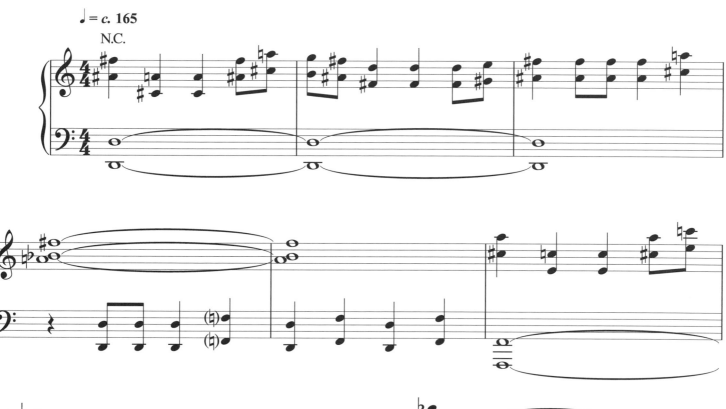

TOMMY: My dad-dy says I'm his spe-cial lit-tle guy...

LAVENDER: I am a prin-cess... And

ERIC: I am a prince...

ALICE: Mum says I'm an an - gel...

AMANDA: Mum says I'm an an - gel...

NIGEL: Mum says I'm an an - gel...

BIG KIDS: And so you think you're a - ble to sur-vive this mess by be - ing a prince or a prin - cess. You will soon

A tempo (♩ = c. 105)

42

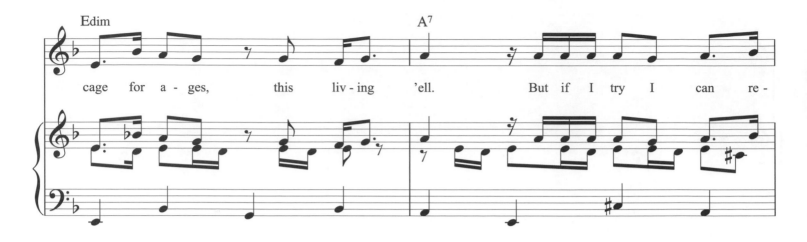

cage for a - ges, this liv - ing 'ell. But if I try I can re -

-mem - ber, back be - fore my life had end - ed, be - fore my hap - py days were

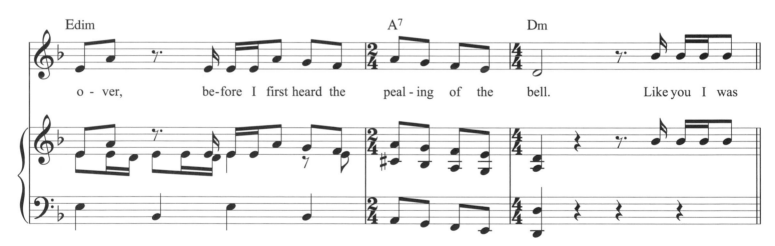

o - ver, be-fore I first heard the peal -ing of the bell. Like you I was

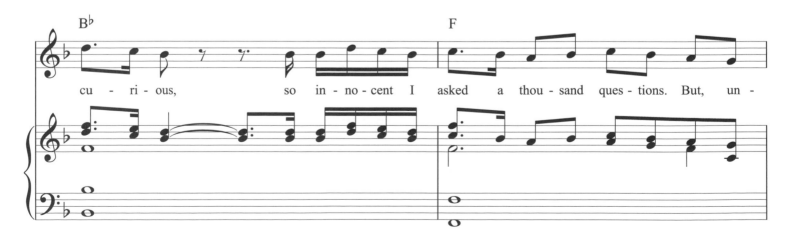

cu - ri - ous, so in -no-cent I asked a thou - sand ques - tions. But, un -

Lyrics:

E♭m · · · F♭maj7(♯11)

A - ble to sur - vive this mess by Be - ing a prince or a prin - cess. You will soon

E♭m · · · B♭ · · · N.C.

(C)see there's no es - cap - ing tra - ge - Dy. And

E♭m · · · F♭maj7(♯11)

E - ven if you put in heaps of eF - fort, you're just wast - ing en - er -

E♭m · · · B♭7 · · · E♭m

-Gy, 'cause your life as you know it is "aitcH"-ent his - to - ry.

I have suf-fered in this Jail.___ Have been trapped in - side this

(K) cage for a - ges, this liv-ing 'eLl. But if I try I can re-

-meM - ber, back be-fore my life had eNd - ed, be-fore my hap - py days were

O - ver, be-fore I first heard the Peal-ing of the bell. Like you I was

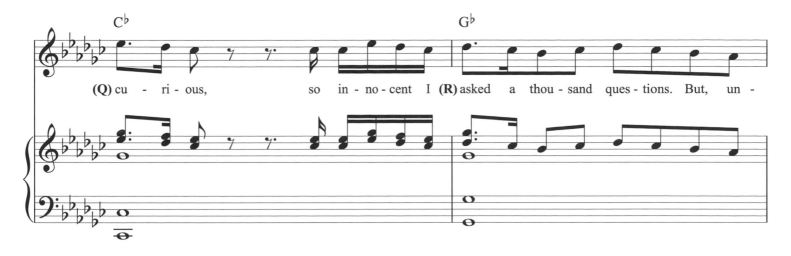

C♭   G♭

(Q) cu - ri - ous,   so in - no - cent I (R) asked a thou - sand ques - tions. But, un -

B♭7(♭9)

-leSs you want to suf - fer, lis - ten up and I will Teach you   a thing or two.

A♭m   E♭m

YoU lis - ten here,   my dear, you'll be pu - nished so se - Vere-ly if you step out of line. And if you cry it will be

B♭7   REGINALD:

(W) dou - ble. You should stay out of trou-ble and re-mem-ber to be   eX-treme-ly care - ful.   WhY?

50

Pathetic

Words & Music by Tim Minchin

Knock on the door, Jen - ny. Just knock on the door. Don't be pa-

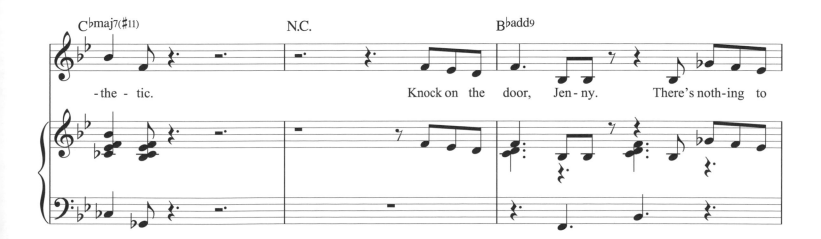

-the - tic. Knock on the door, Jen - ny. There's noth - ing to

© Copyright 2011 Navel Enterprises Pty Ltd.
Kobalt Music Publishing Limited.
Print rights for the world exclusively administered by Music Sales Limited.
All Rights Reserved. International Copyright Secured.

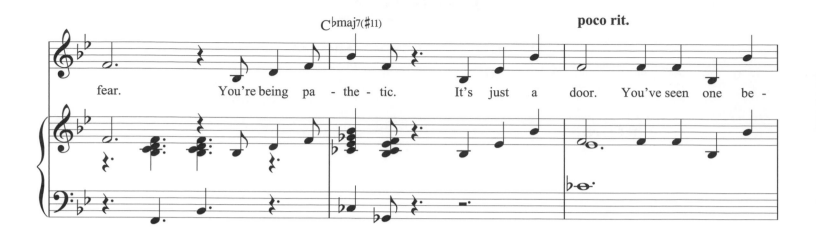

fear. You're being pa - the - tic. It's just a door. You've seen one be -

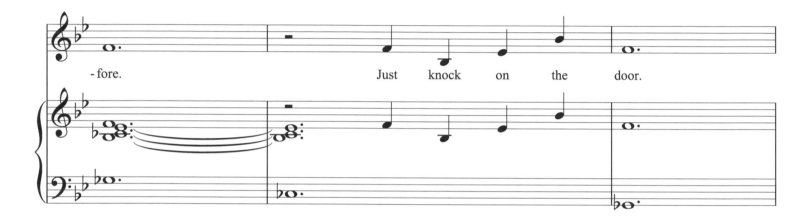

-fore. Just knock on the door.

Look at you try - ing to hide, sil - ly. Stand - ing out -

-side the prin - ci - ple's of - fice like a lit - tle____ girl.__

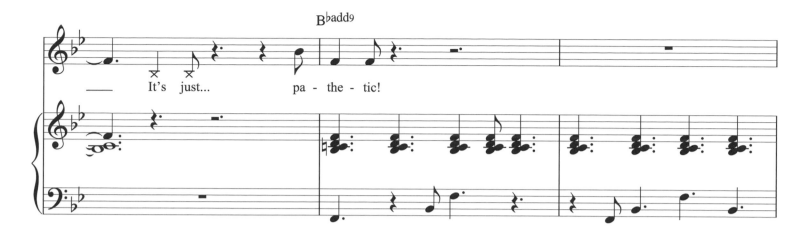

It's just... pa - the - tic!

Look at you he - si - tat - ing, hands shak - ing.

You should be em - bar - rassed. You're not a lit - tle girl.

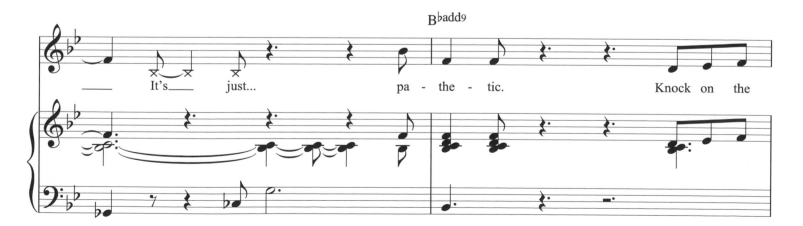

It's just... pa - the - tic. Knock on the

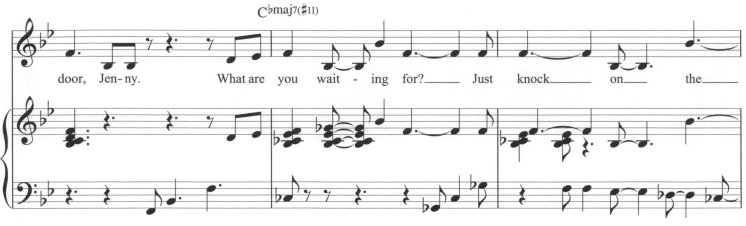

C♭maj7(♯11)

door, Jen- ny. What are you wait - ing for?_____ Just knock_____ on_____ the_____

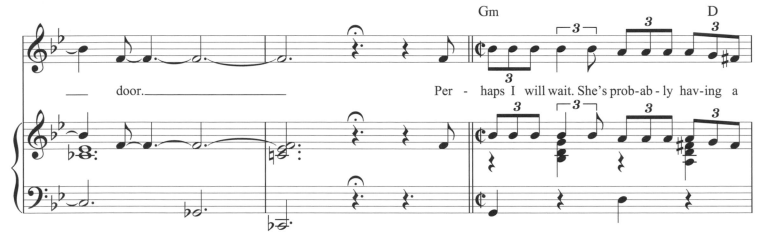

_____ door._____

Fast 2

Gm   D

Per - haps I will wait. She's prob-ab-ly hav-ing a

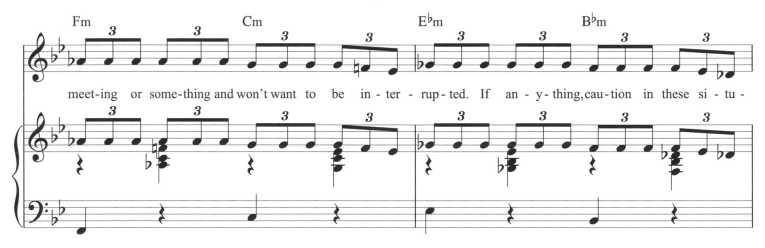

Fm   Cm   E♭m   B♭m

meet-ing or some-thing and won't want to be in - ter - rup-ted. If an - y-thing, cau-tion in these si - tu -

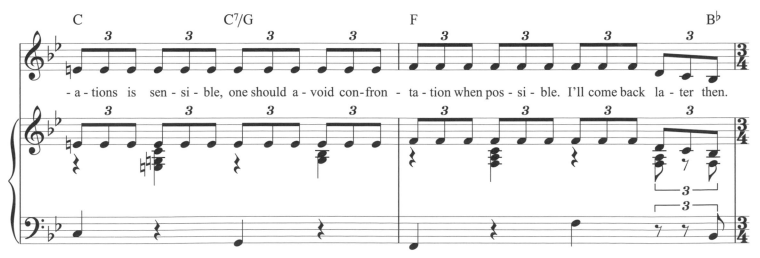

C   C7/G   F   B♭

- a - tions is sen - si - ble, one should a - void con-fron - ta - tion when pos - si - ble. I'll come back la - ter then.

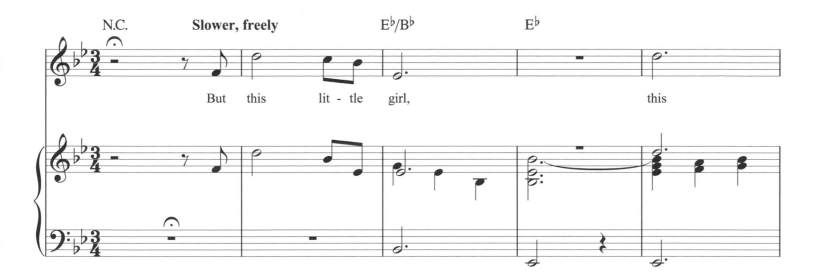

But this lit - tle girl, this

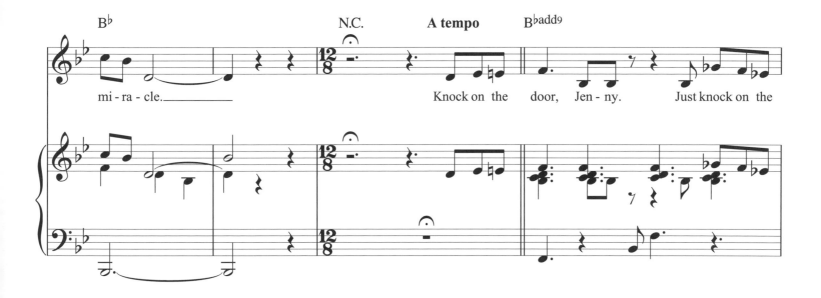

mi - ra - cle._____ Knock on the door, Jen - ny. Just knock on the

door. Don't be pa - the - tic!

(Knocks)

2

55

The Hammer

Words & Music by Tim Minchin

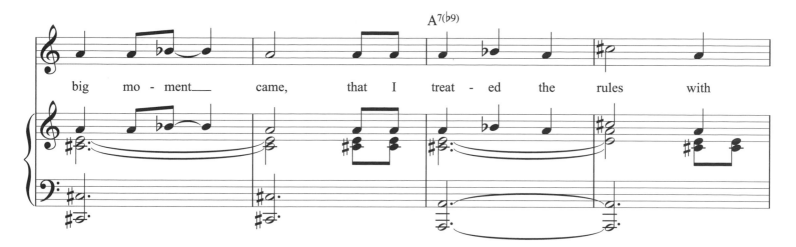

big mo - ment___ came, that I treat - ed the rules with

cas - ual dis - dain? Well? Like hell!

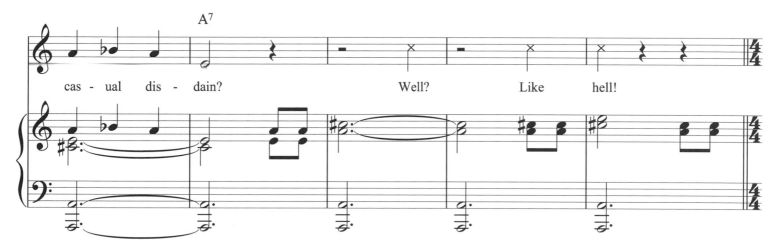

As I stepped up to the cir - cle, did I change my plan? Huh?___ What? As I chalked up my

palms, did I wave my hands? I did not! As I start - ed my

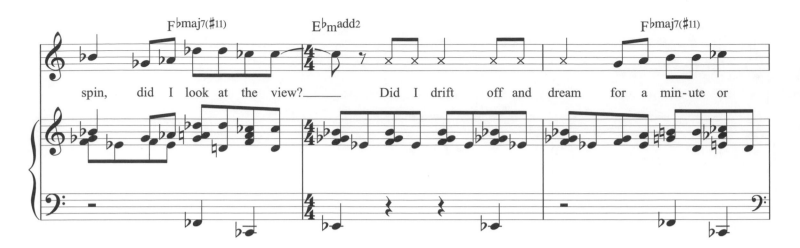

spin, did I look at the view?_____ Did I drift off and dream for a min-ute or

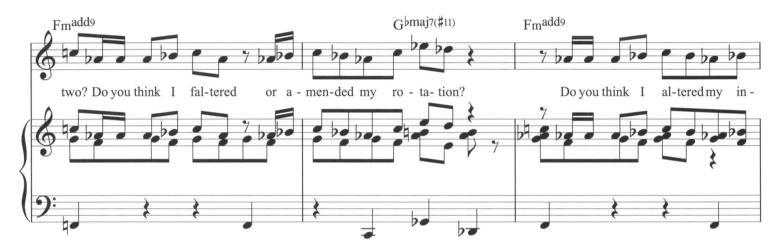

two? Do you think I fal-tered or a-men-ded my ro-ta-tion? Do you think I al-tered my in-

-ten-ded el-e-va - tion? As the ham-mer took off, did I change my

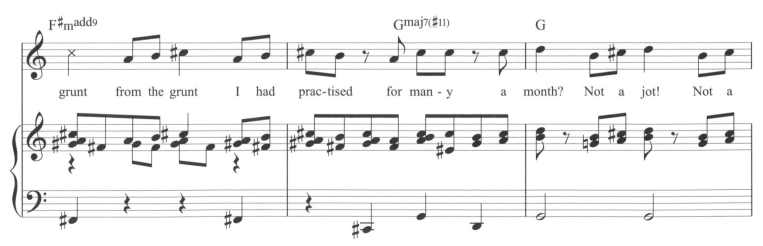

grunt from the grunt I had prac-tised for man-y a month? Not a jot! Not a

dot did I stray from the plot! Not a de-tail of my throw was ad-jus-ted or for-

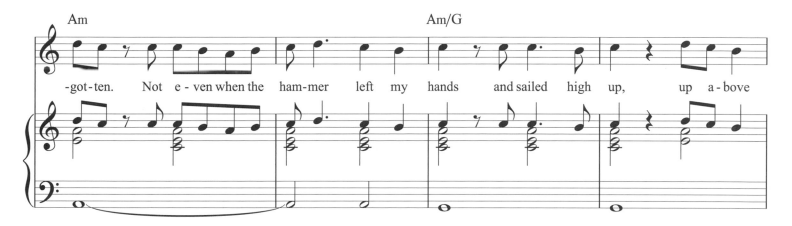

-got-ten. Not e-ven when the ham-mer left my hands and sailed high up, up a-bove

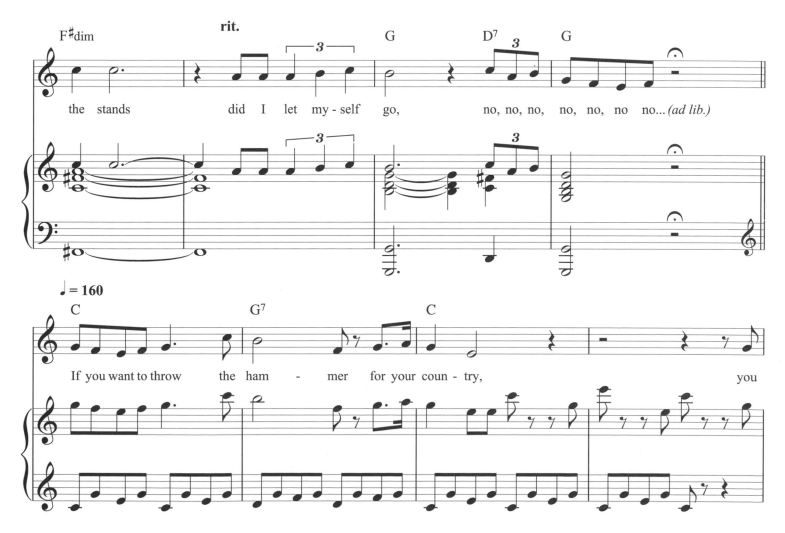

the stands did I let my-self go, no, no, no, no, no, no no... *(ad lib.)*

If you want to throw the ham - mer for your coun-try, you

have to stay in-side the cir - cle all the time.

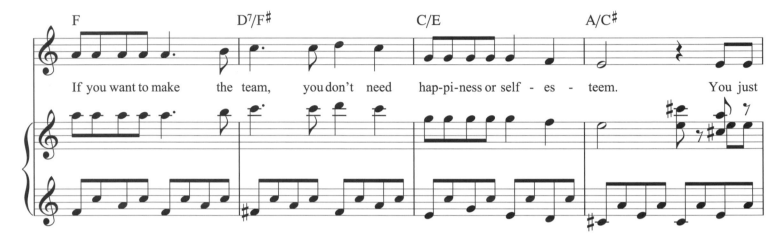

If you want to make the team, you don't need hap-pi-ness or self - es - teem. You just

need to keep your feet in-side the line.
Spoken: Sing, children! Two, three, four!

If you want to throw the ham - mer for your coun - try.
(Bam - bi - na - tum est ma - gi - tum.) You

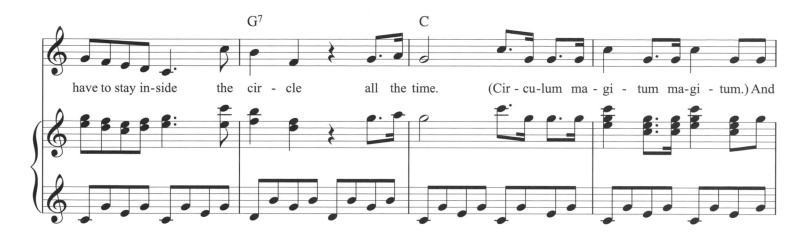

have to stay in-side the cir - cle all the time. (Cir - cu-lum ma - gi - tum ma-gi - tum.) And

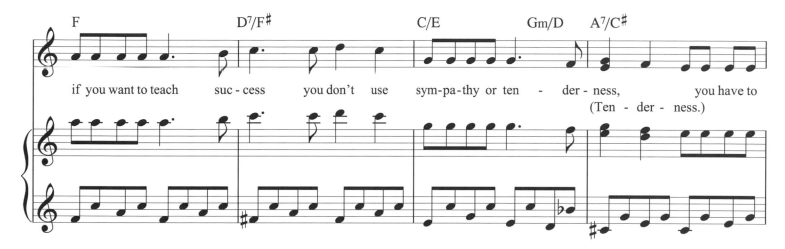

if you want to teach suc - cess you don't use sym-pa-thy or ten - der - ness, you have to
(Ten - der - ness.)

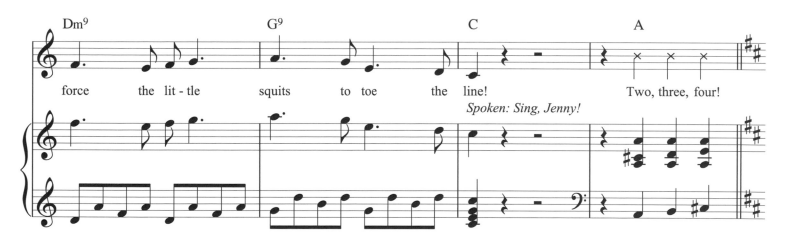

force the lit - tle squits to toe the line! Two, three, four!
Spoken: Sing, Jenny!

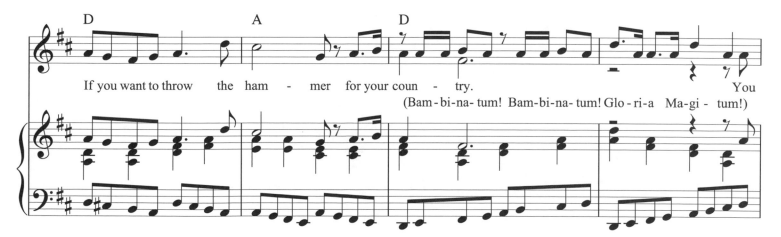

If you want to throw the ham - mer for your coun - try. You
(Bam - bi-na- tum! Bam-bi-na- tum! Glo - ri-a Ma-gi - tum!)

have to stay in-side   the cir-cle   all the time.   I ap-
                                            (Cir - cu-lum est De - us! De - us!)

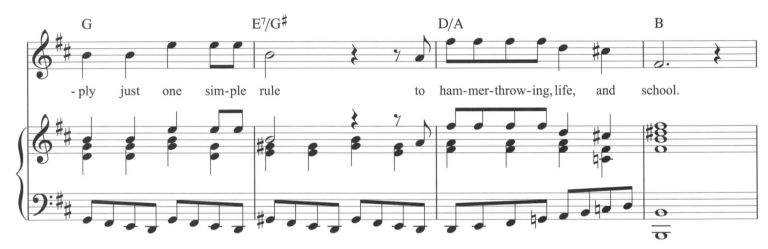

-ply   just   one sim-ple rule   to ham-mer-throw-ing, life,   and   school.

Life's   a ball,   so   learn   to throw it,   find   the bal-ly

line   and toe it,   and al - ways keep your   feet   in-side   the   line.

Spoken: Now get out!

Loud

Words & Music by Tim Minchin

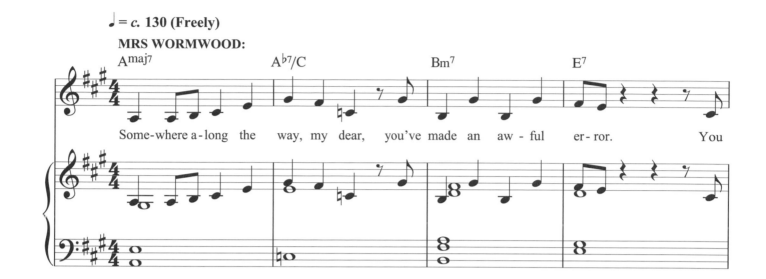

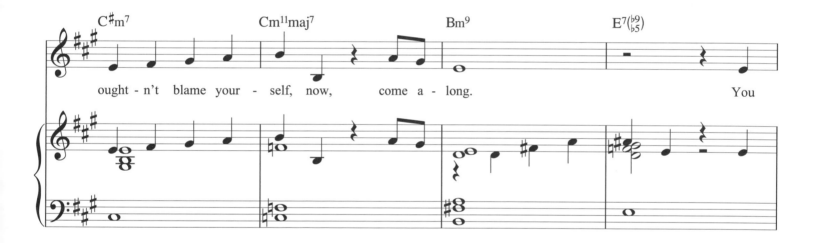

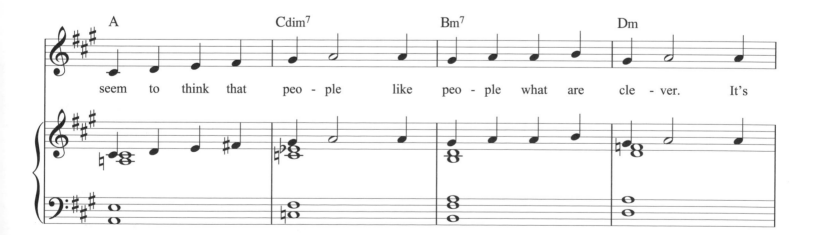

ver - y quaint,__ it's ver - y sweet,__ but wrong.

Peo - ple don't like smart - y pants__ what go 'round claim - ing that they

know stuff we don't know.

Spoken: Now here's a tip:

What you know__ mat - ters less__

__ than the vol - ume with which what you don't know's ex - pressed. Con - tent has nev - er been less__

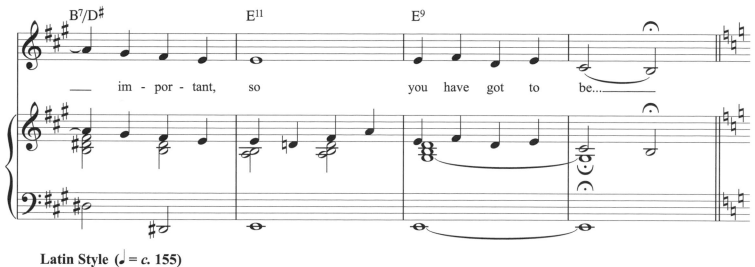

im - por - tant, so you have got to be...

Latin Style (♩ = c. 155)

Loud! (Loud,_ loud!)__ Girl, you got-ta learn to stand up and stick out__ from the

crowd! (Crowd,_ crowd!)__ A lit - tle less

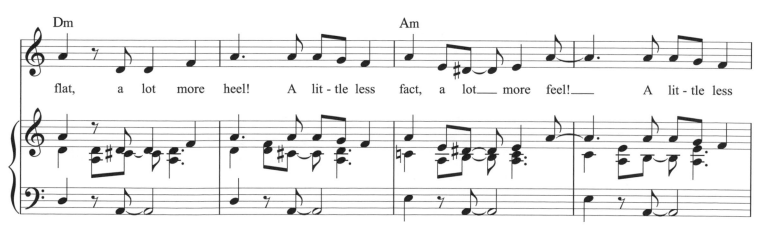

flat, a lot more heel! A lit - tle less fact, a lot__ more feel!__ A lit - tle less

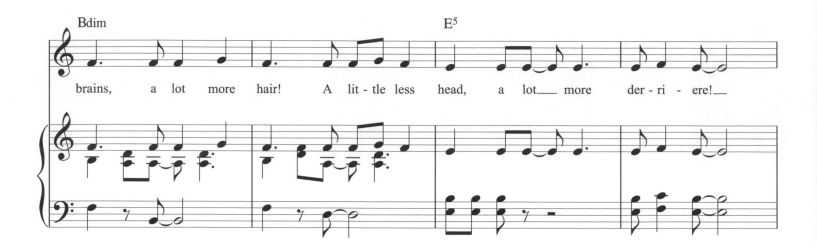

Bdim   E⁵

brains, a lot more hair! A lit - tle less head, a lot___ more der - ri - ere!___

N.C.

Am^add9

No one's gon - na tell you when to shake your tush.___ Well, you got a light; don't hide it

E⁷

un - der a bush - el. No___ one's gon - na look if you don't___ stand out.___ No___

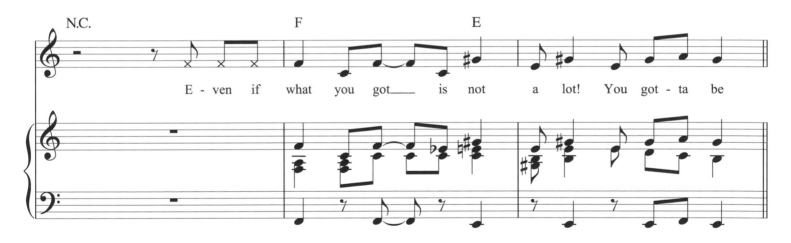

Am   F⁷   E⁷

proud! (Proud,__ proud!)__   A lit - tle less

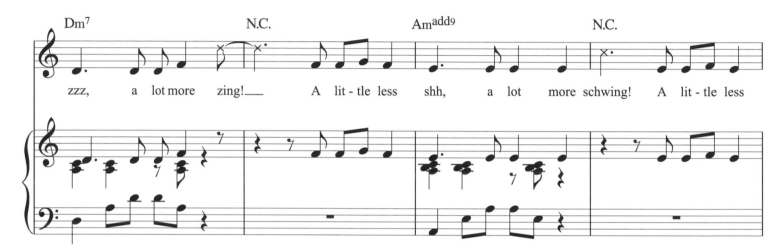

Dm⁷   N.C.   Am^add9   N.C.

zzz,   a lot more zing!__ A lit - tle less shh, a lot more schwing! A lit - tle less

Bm⁷⁽♭⁵⁾   E⁵

dress - ing like__ your mum, a lit - tle more bum - ba, bom - bom - ba - da - bom!_

N.C.

No one's gon-na tell you when to wig-gle your bum - ba. No one's gon-na love you if you don't know the rum - ba.

MRS WORMWOOD:

RUDOLPHO:

MRS WORMWOOD:

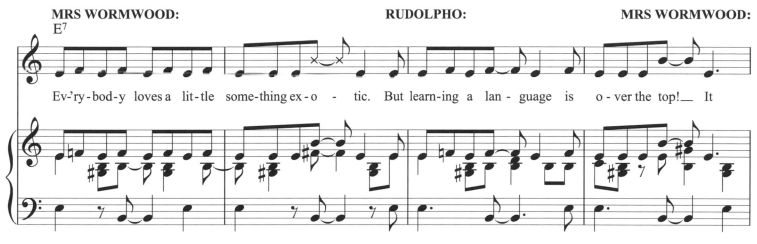

Ev-'ry-bod-y loves a lit-tle some-thing ex-o - tic. But learn-ing a lan-guage is o-ver the top!__ It

RUDOLPHO:

does-n't real-ly mat-ter if you don't know nowt!__ As long as you don't know it with a

MRS WORMWOOD AND RUDOLPHO:

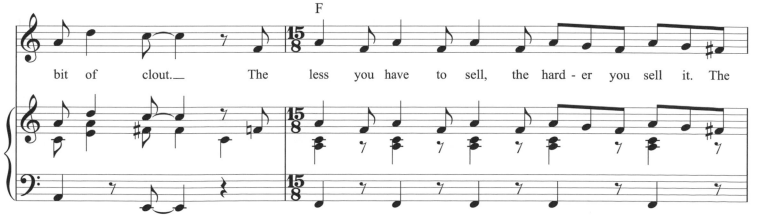

bit of clout.__ The less you have to sell, the hard-er you sell it. The

less you have to say, the loud-er you yell it. The dumb-er the act, the big - ger the con - fes-sion. The

less you have to show, the loud-er you dress it. You got-ta get up. You got-ta get up___ and be

loud! (Loud, loud!)___ You got-ta give your-self per-mis-sion to shine and stick out___ from the

MRS WORMWOOD:

crowd! (Crowd, crowd!)___ A lit - tle less...

A lit - tle more... A lit - tle less...

A lit - tle more!

No one's gon-na tell you when to oh, oh, oh! No one's gon-na show you where to huh, huh, huh!

71

If you want a lit-tle bit of mm, mm, mm... *Spoken: You can't sit around going*

la, la, la! No one's gon-na care if you___ don't care,___ so

go and put some_high-lights in your hair.___ 'Cause you got-ta high-light what you got!

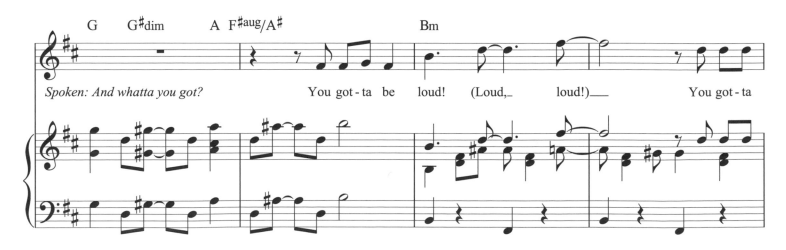

Spoken: And whatta you got? You got-ta be loud! (Loud,___ loud!)___ You got-ta

give your-self per-mis-sion to shine,___ stick out___ from the crowd! (Crowd,___ crowd!)___

___ You got-ta be

loud, loud,___ loud,___ loud,___

RUDOLPHO:

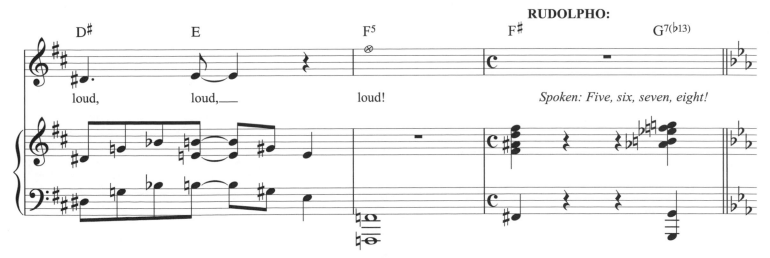

loud, loud,___ loud!

Spoken: Five, six, seven, eight!

73

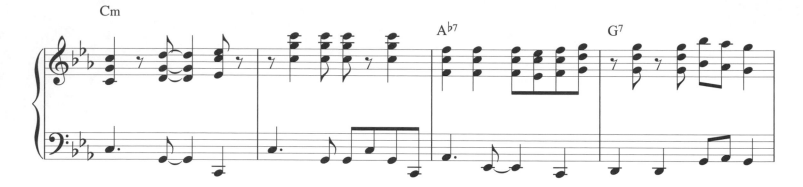

MRS WORMWOOD:

You got-ta be

loud! (Loud,____ loud!)____ And stick out____ from the

crowd! (Crowd, crowd!)____ You got - ta be

loud! Stand up____ and be

75

proud, proud, proud, proud!

Loud, loud,— loud,— loud,— loud, loud,— loud,—

— loud,— loud,— loud,— loud,— loud....

You got-ta be LOUD!

This Little Girl

Words & Music by Tim Minchin

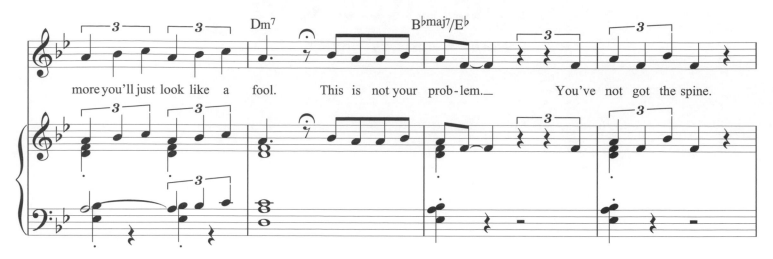

more you'll just look like a fool. This is not your prob-lem.___ You've not got the spine.

You are a tea-cher. Just go back to school! But this lit-tle

girl, this mi-ra-cle. She seems not to know___ that she's spe-cial at all.___

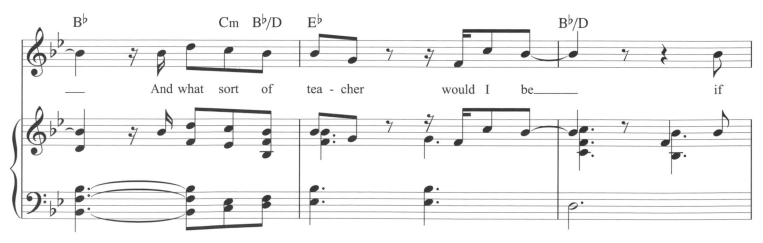

___ And what sort of tea-cher would I be___ if

I let this lit - tle girl fall? I can see this lit - tle girl

needs some - bod - y strong to fight by her side. In - stead she's found

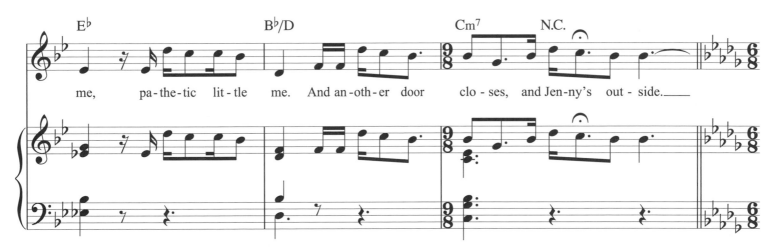

me, pa - the - tic lit - tle me. And an - oth - er door clo - ses, and Jen - ny's out - side.

Bruce

Words & Music by Tim Minchin

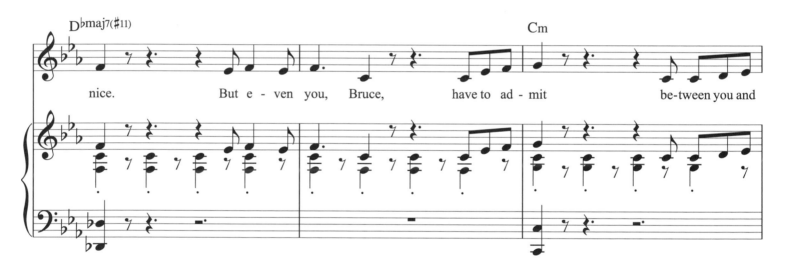

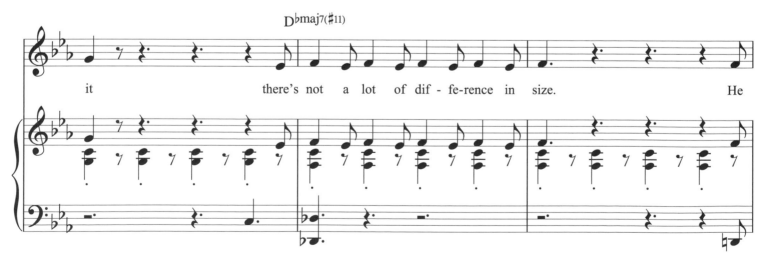

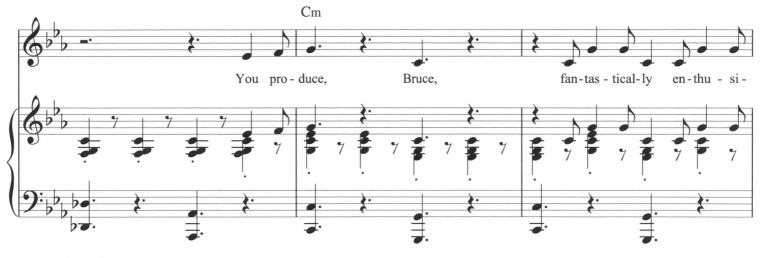

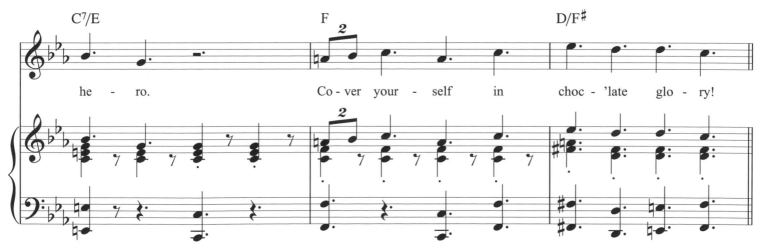

Bruce!
You'll nev-er a-gain be sub-ject to a-buse for your im-

-mense ca-boose! She'll call a truce, Bruce. With ev-'ry swal-low you are

tight-en-ing the noose. We nev-er thought it was pos-si-ble,

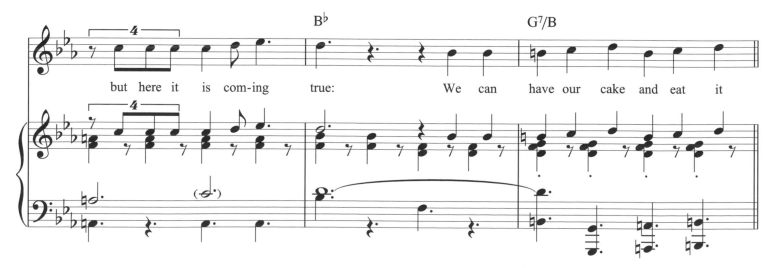

but here it is com-ing true: We can have our cake and eat it

Come on,___ Bruce,___ be our he - ro. Co-ver your-self in choc - 'late

glo - ry... *Whispered: Go on Bruce. Do it!* Oh...

Bruce! You'll nev-er a-gain be sub-ject to a-buse for your im-

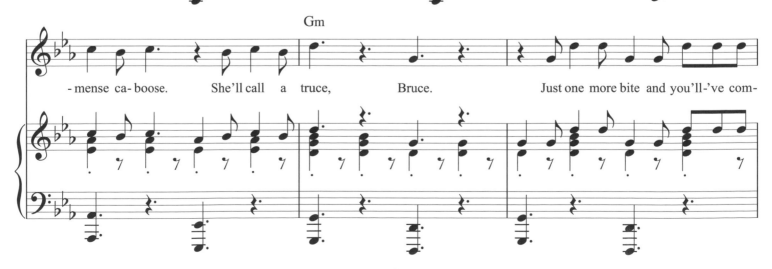

-mense ca-boose. She'll call a truce, Bruce. Just one more bite and you'll-'ve com-

- plete - ly cooked her goose.   We nev - er thought it was pos - si - ble,

but here it is com - ing true: We can have our cake and eat it...

Ah,_____   ah,_____

ah,_____   ah!_____

Telly

Words & Music by Tim Minchin

If you know a thing al-read-y, ba-by, you can switch the chan-nel o-ver just like that!
I was pret-ty smart al-read-y, but now I'm real-ly, real-ly smart, ver-y, ver-y smart.

End-less joy and end-less laugh - ter, folks liv-in' hap-pi-ly ev-er af - ter,
End-less con-tent, end-less chan-nels, end-less___ chat on end-less pan - els,

all you need___ to make you wise,___ is twen-ty-three mi-nutes plus ad-ver-tise-ments.
all you need___ to fill your muf-fin with - out hav-ing to real-ly fink or nuff - in._____

Why would we waste our en-er-gy turn-ing the pa-ges one, two, three? When
Why would we waste our en-er-gy try-ing to work out U - lys-ses? When

Who the dick-ens is Charles Dick-ens? Mar-y Shel-ley? Cor, she sounds smell-y.

Har-ry Pot-ter? What a rot-ter! Jane Aus-ten, in the com-post-in! James Joyce does-n't sound noice!

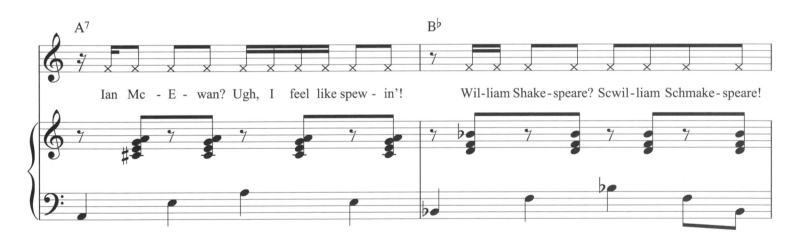

Ian Mc-E-wan? Ugh, I feel like spew-in'! Wil-liam Shake-speare? Scwil-liam Schmake-speare!

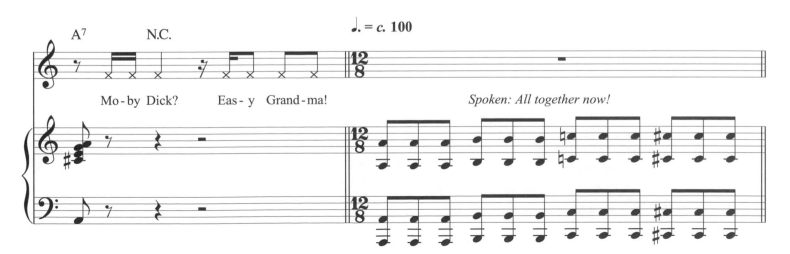

Mo-by Dick? Eas-y Grand-ma! *Spoken: All together now!*

All I know_ I learnt from_ tel - ly. The big-ger the tel - ly, the

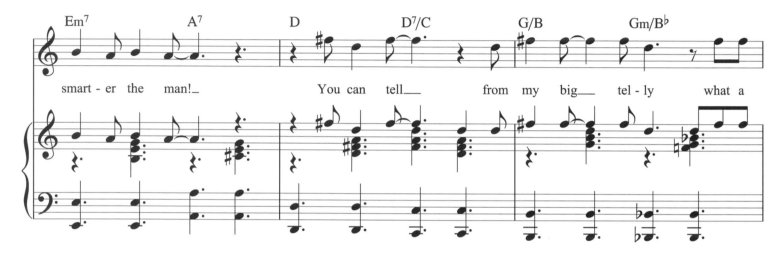

smart - er the man!_ You can tell_ from my big_ tel - ly what a

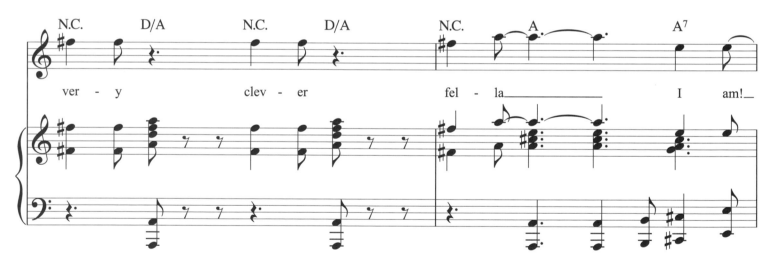

ver - y clev - er fel - la_____ I am!_

When I Grow Up

Words & Music by Tim Minchin

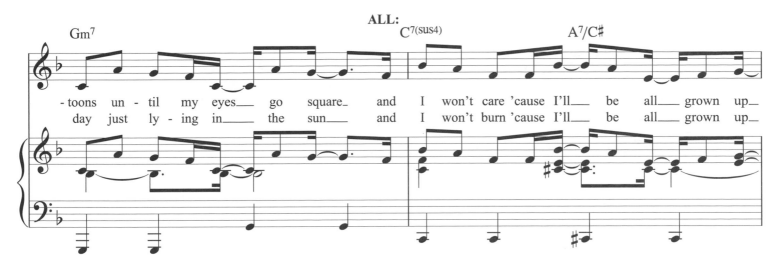

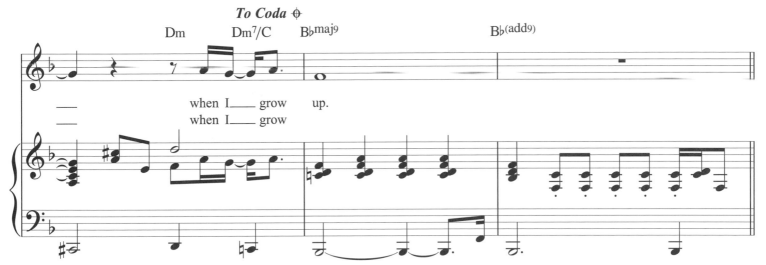

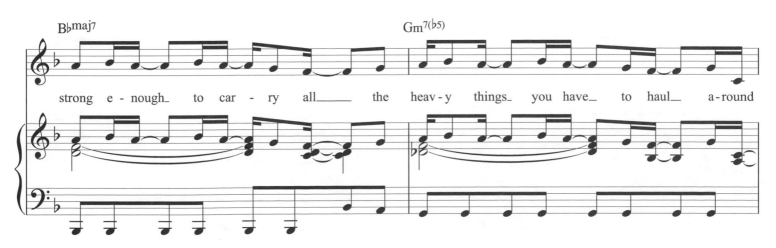

with you___ when you're a grown up.___

And when I grow up,___ (When I grow up, when I grow up.) I will be

brave e-nough to fight___ the crea-tures that you have to fight___ be-neath___ the bed

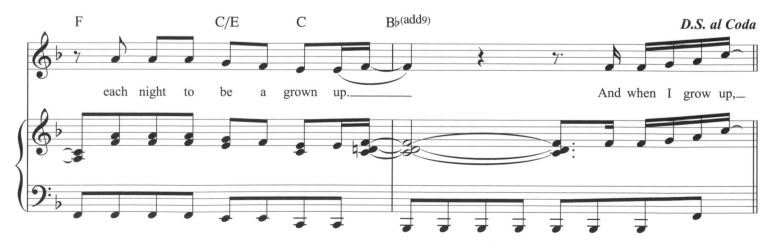

each night to be a grown up.___ And when I grow up,___

D.S. al Coda

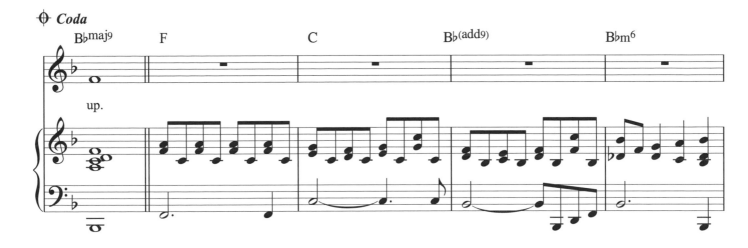

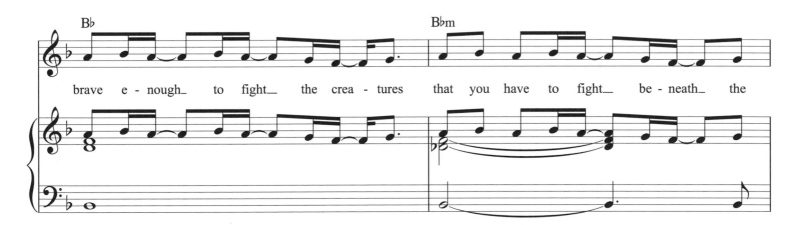

I'm Here

Words & Music by Tim Minchin

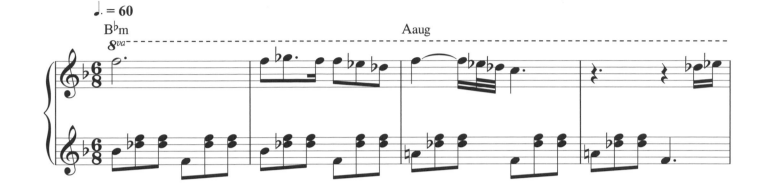

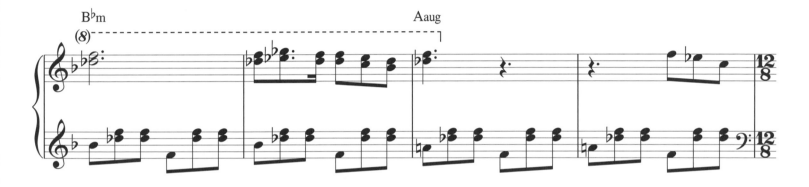

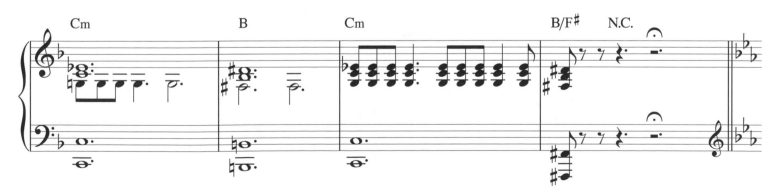

Don't

cry, I am here, lit-tle girl._____ Please don't

cry. Dry your eyes. Wipe a-way your tears,_____ lit-tle girl._____ For-

-give me._____ I did-n't mean to de-sert you._____ Don't

cry, lit-tle girl. Noth-ing can hurt you. You've noth-ing to

fear. I'm here.

Spoken Interlude

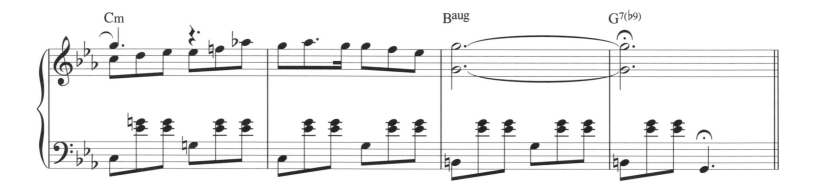

Slower

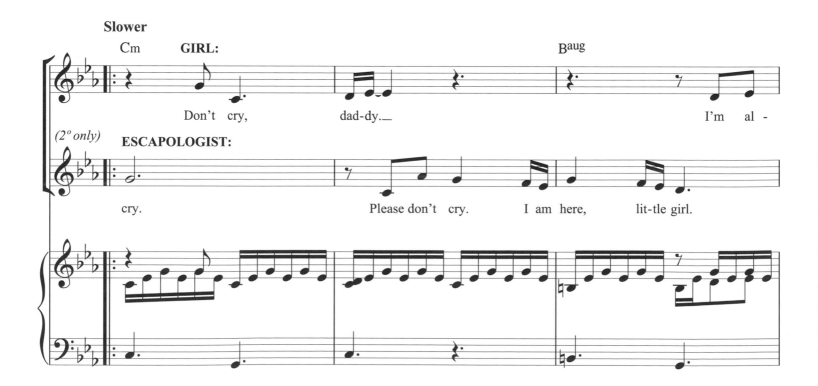

(2° only)

ESCAPOLOGIST:

GIRL: Don't cry, dad-dy.__ I'm al-

cry. Please don't cry. I am here, lit-tle girl.

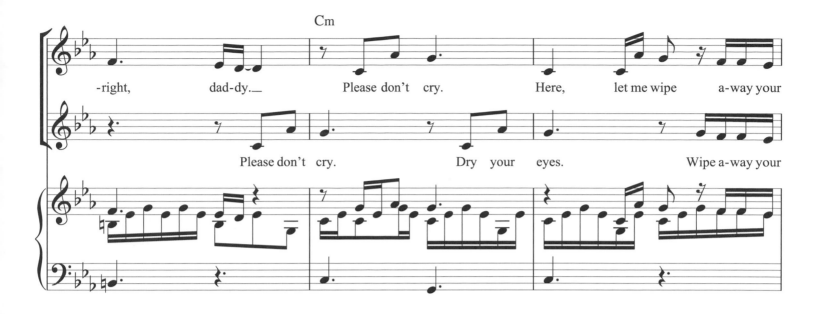

Cm

-right,   dad-dy.__   Please don't cry.   Here,   let me wipe a-way your

Please don't cry.   Dry   your   eyes.   Wipe a-way your

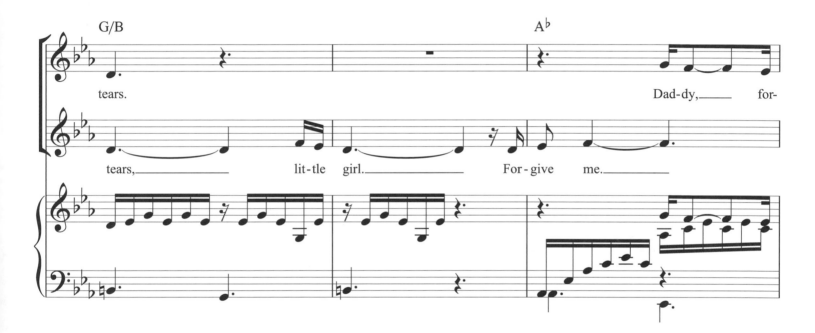

G/B   A♭

tears.   Dad-dy,_____   for-

tears,_____   lit-tle girl._____   For-give   me._____

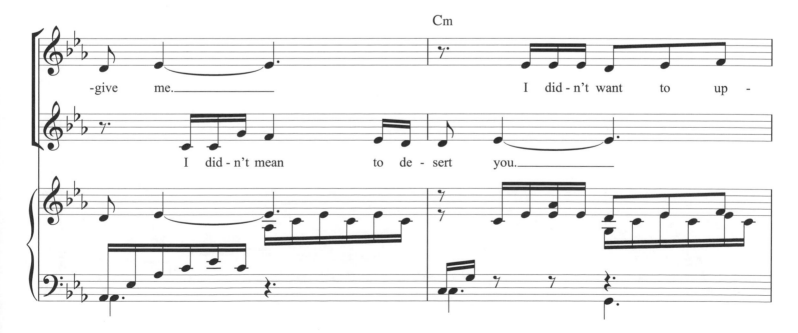

Cm

-give   me._____   I   did-n't want   to   up-

I did-n't mean   to de - sert   you._____

Spoken Interlude

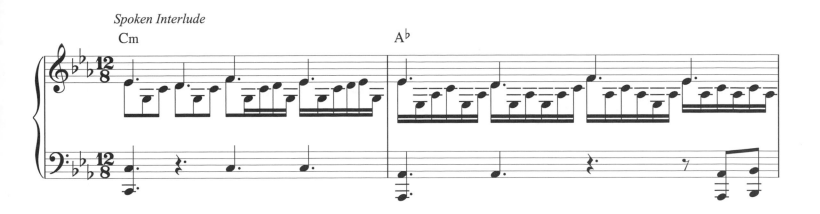

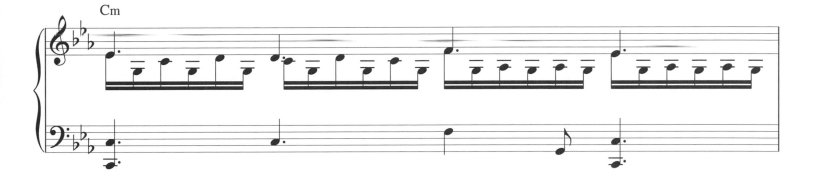

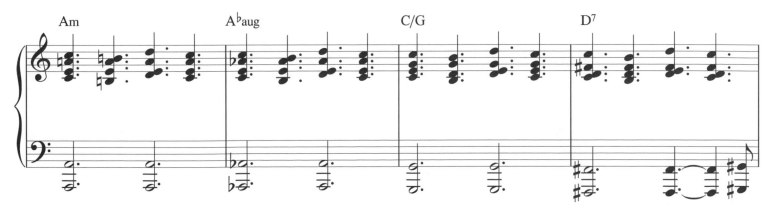

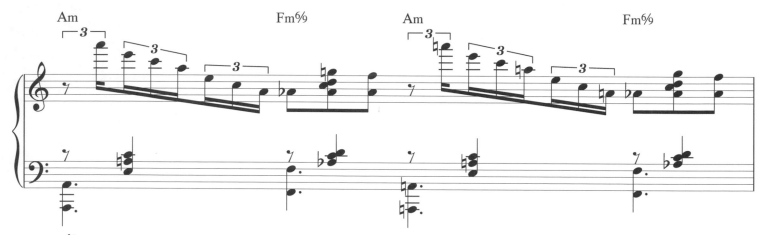

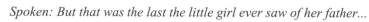

Spoken: But that was the last the little girl ever saw of her father...

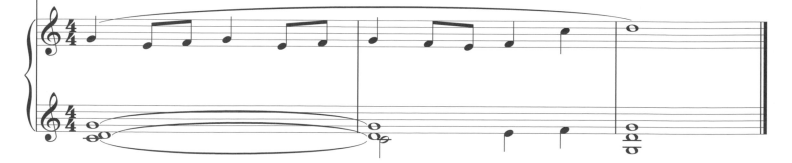

The Smell Of Rebellion

Words & Music by Tim Minchin

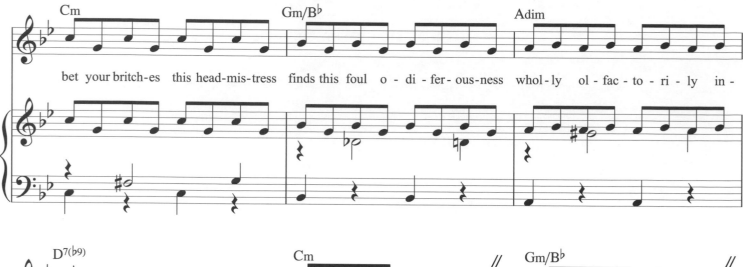

bet your britch-es this head-mis-tress finds this foul o - di - fer - ous-ness whol - ly ol - fac - to - ri - ly in-

-sult - ing.   And   so, to stop the stench's spread, I   find   a   ses - sion of Phys-Ed

sorts the mere - ly rank from the re - volt - ing.___   The smell of re - bel-

Slight Swing ($\bullet$ = *c.* 120)

- lion comes out in the sweat___   and Phys - Ed will get you sweat - ing.   And it won't be

Am   **E⁷/B**   **Am/C**   **E⁷/D**   **F⁷**

-fi - ance, the o - dour of coup,— the waft of an - arch - y in pro -

E⁷   **Dm**   **Am**

- gress. Once we've ex - er - cised these de - mons, they shall be too pooped for dream - in'. Some

B⁷   *rit.*   **E⁷**

dou - ble - time dis - ci - pline should stop the rot from set - ting in. One, two, three, four!

Spoken: All right, let's step it up.
Double-time!

A tempo (Straight ♪=♩)

Am

Dis - cip - line, dis - cip - line for child - ren who aren't lis - ten - ing, for

midgets who are fidgeting and whispering in history. Their chattering and chittering, their nattering and twittering is tempered with a smattering of discipline. We must begin insisting on rigidity and discipline, persistently resisting this anarchistic mischiefin'. These minutes you are fritterin' on pandering and pitying while

-volt, the reek of pre - pu-bes-cent plot-ting. The whiff of re-sis-tance, the pong of dis-

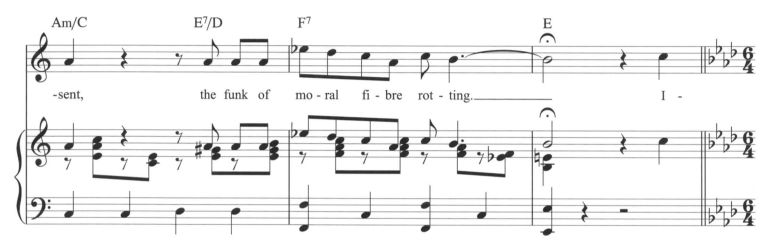

-sent, the funk of mo-ral fi-bre rot-ting._____ I -

♩. = c. 65 (Ballad tempo)

-ma-gine a world_ with no child-ren. Close your eyes_ and just

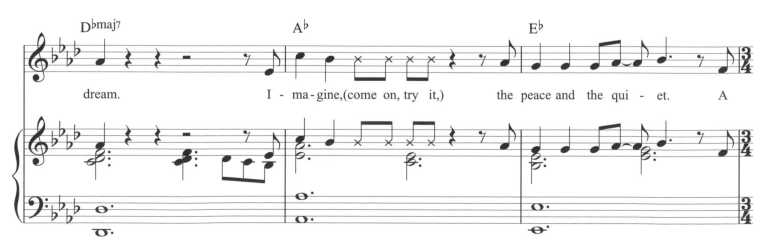

dream. I-ma-gine,(come on, try it,) the peace and the qui-et. A

114

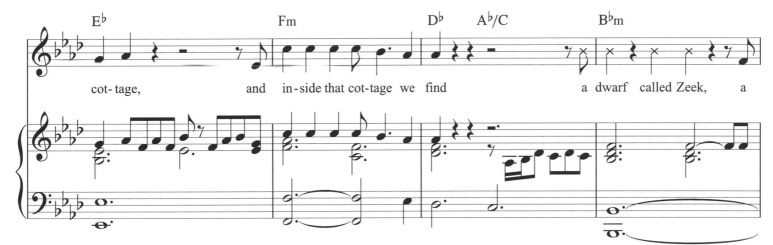

-way.   If you find your way_ through,_ they'll be wait-ing for you,_ sing - ing..."

Freely

Spoken: Neigh, neigh!

Eric: She's mad!

A - ha! And there, just like I said, the stink-y mag-got rears his head.

♩ = c. 95

E - ven the squit-ti - est, pit-e-ous mess can har - bour seeds of stink-i - ness. Have you

ev-er seen an-y-thing more re-pel-lent? Have you ev - er smelled an-y-thing worse than that smell of re-

Swing (♩ = *c.* 100)

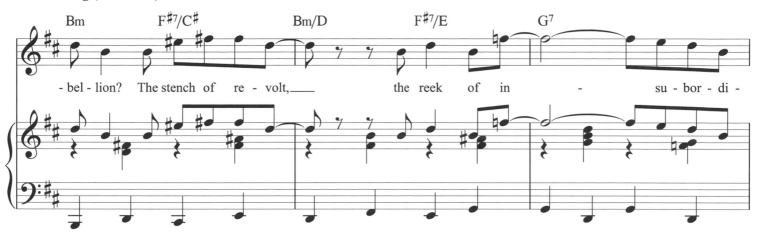

-bel - lion? The stench of re - volt,___ the reek of in - su - bor - di -

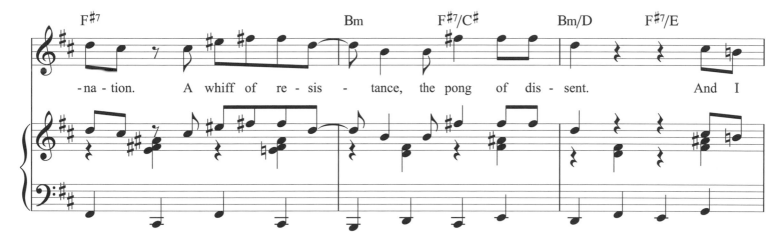

-na - tion. A whiff of re - sis - tance, the pong of dis - sent. And I

will not stop till you are squashed. Till this re - bel - li - on is quashed. Till glo - rious, sweat-y dis - ci - pline has

washed this sick-en-ing scent a - way!___

Quiet

Words & Music by Tim Minchin

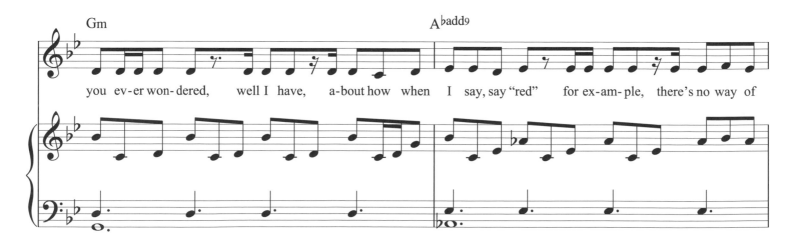

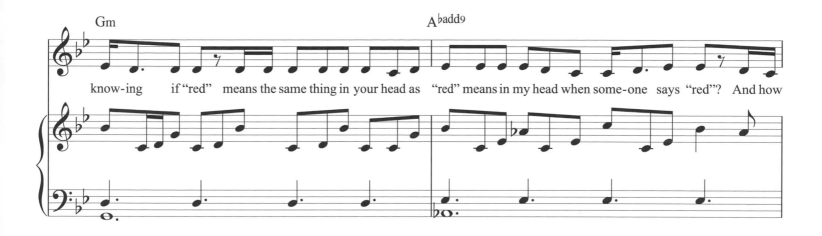

know-ing if "red" means the same thing in your head as "red" means in my head when some-one says "red"? And how

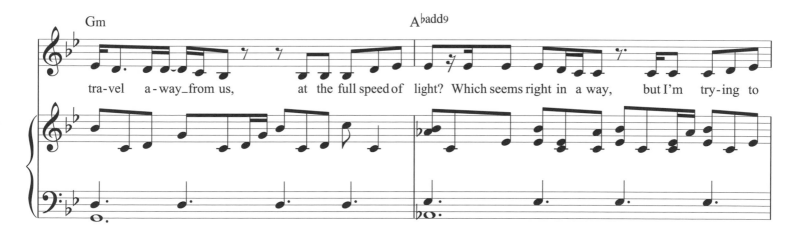

if we are tra-vel-ling at al-most the speed of light and we're hold-ing a light, that light would still

tra-vel a-way from us, at the full speed of light? Which seems right in a way, but I'm try-ing to

say, I'm not sure, but I won-der if in-side my head, I'm not just a bit diff-'rent from some of my

friends. These ans-wers that come in - to my mind un - bid-den. These sto - ries de - li - vered to me ful - ly

writ - ten. And when ev-'ry-one shouts like they seem to like_ shout-ing, the noise in my head is in - cre-dib - ly loud

and I just wish they'd stop, my dad and my mum, and the tel-ly and sto-ries would stop for just

once. And I'm sor-ry I'm not quite ex-plain-ing it right,___ but this noise be-comes an - ger, and the an-ger is

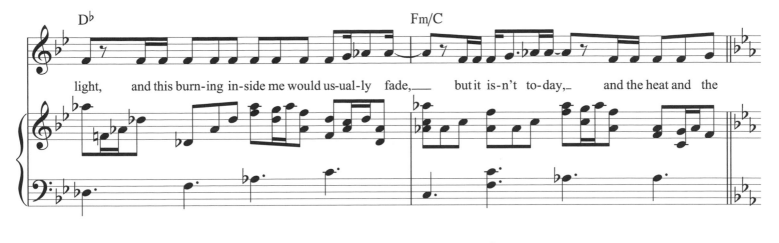

light,   and this burn-ing in-side me would us-ual-ly fade,___   but it is-n't to-day,___   and the heat and the

shout-ing,   and my heart is pound-ing,   and my eyes   are   burn-ing,   and sud-den - ly

ev-'ry- thing, ev-'ry-thing is...   Qui-et.   Like si- lence, but not real-ly

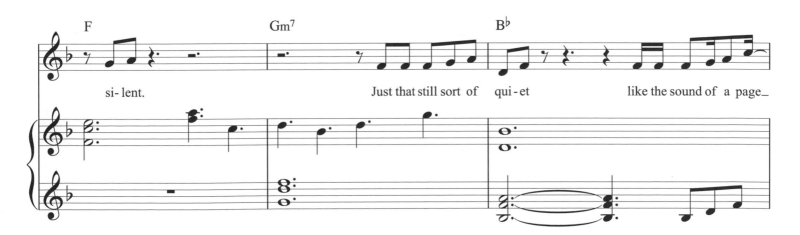

si- lent.   Just that still sort of   qui-et   like the sound of a page___

being turned in a book, or a pause in a walk in the woods.

Qui - et.

Like si - lence, but not real - ly

si - lent.

Just that nice kind of qui - et

like the sound when you

lie up-side down in your bed.

Just the sound of your heart in your head.

And though the

people a-round me, their mouths are still mov - ing, the words they are forming can-not reach me an-y-more. And it is qui-et and I am warm like I've sailed in - to the eye of the storm.

My House

Words & Music by Tim Minchin

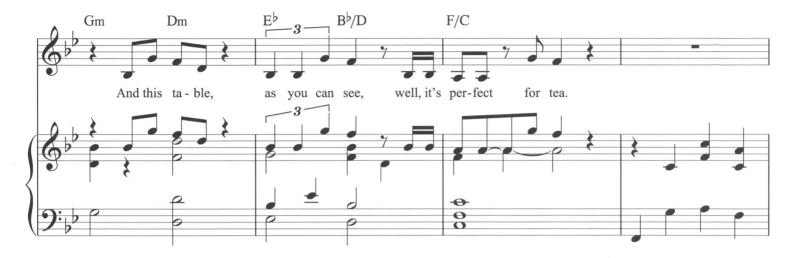

And this ta - ble, as you can see, well, it's per-fect for tea.

It is-n't much,_ but it is__ e-nough for me.

It is - n't much, but it is__ e - nough.

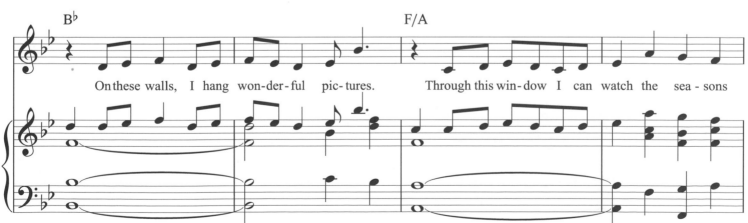

On these walls, I hang won-der-ful pic-tures. Through this win-dow I can watch the sea - sons

change. By this lamp I can read, and I, I am set free!

And when it's cold out-side, I feel no fear, e-ven in the win-ter

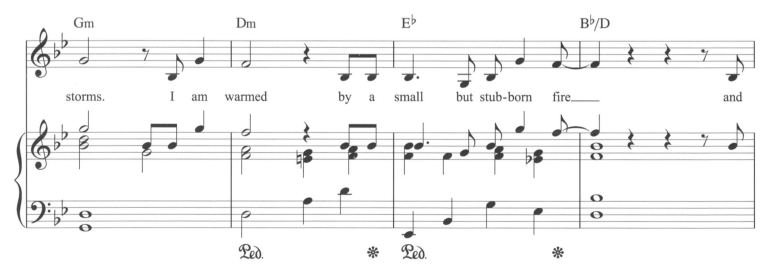

storms. I am warmed by a small but stub-born fire and

there is no-where I would ra-ther be.

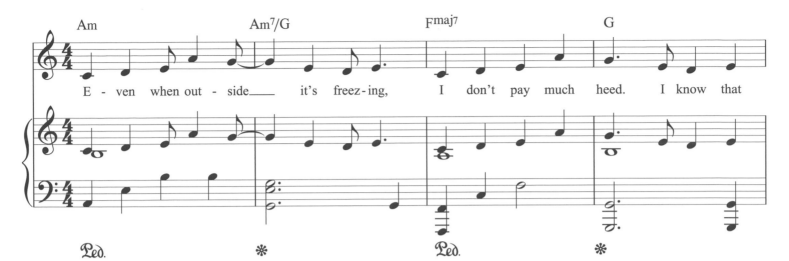

Even when out-side___ it's freez-ing, I don't pay much heed. I know that

ev - 'ry - thing I need___ is in___ here.

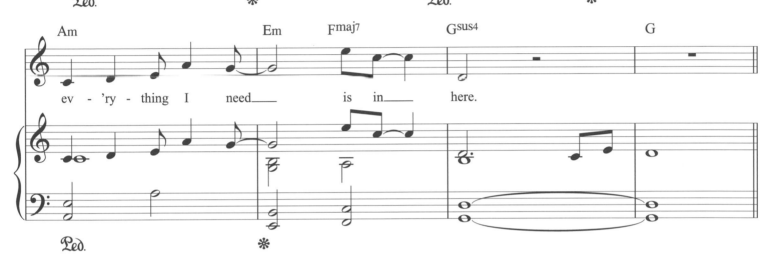

It is - n't much, but it is___ e-nough for me.

poco rit.

It is - n't much, but it is___ e-nough for me.

Revolting Children

Words & Music by Tim Minchin

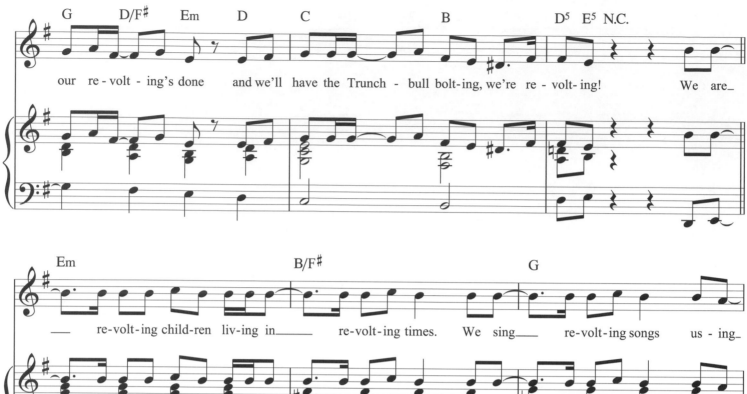

our re-volt-ing's done and we'll have the Trunch-bull bolt-ing, we're re-volt-ing! We are_

_ re-volt-ing child-ren liv-ing in_ re-volt-ing times. We sing_ re-volt-ing songs us-ing_

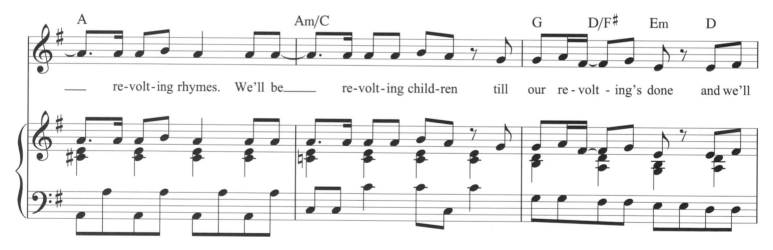

_ re-volt-ing rhymes. We'll be_ re-volt-ing child-ren till our re-volt-ing's done and we'll

TOMMY:

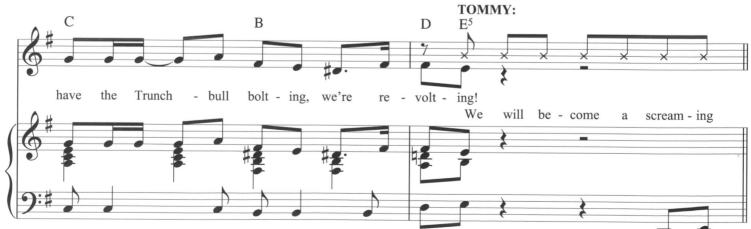

have the Trunch-bull bolt-ing, we're re-volt-ing!

We will be-come a scream-ing

right! Ev -'ry - one! N - O - R - T - WHY?   'Cause we're a lit - tle bit naugh - ty!

You say we ough - ta stay in - side the   line. But if we dis - o - bey at the same

time, there is noth - ing that the Trunch - bull can   do! She can take her ham - mer and S - H -

- U...
You did - n't think you could push us too far,   but there's no go - ing back now, we

R - E - V - O - L - T - I - N. We'll S -

- I - N - G,_____ U - S - I - N - G._____ We'll be_____

_____ R - E - V - O - L - T - I - N - G._____ It is

2 - L - 8 - 4 - U E - R - E - volt - ing! We are_____

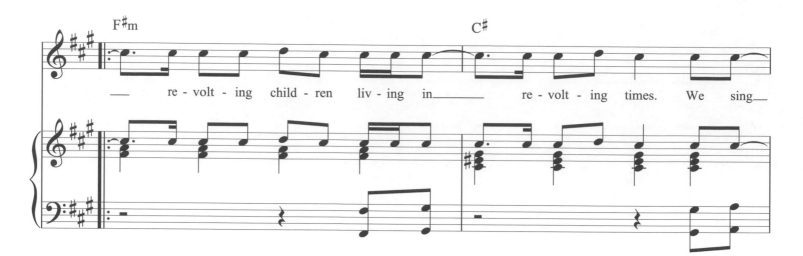

re - volt - ing child - ren liv - ing in____ re - volt - ing times. We sing____

re - volt - ing songs us - ing____ re - volt - ing rhymes. We'll be____

re - volt - ing child - ren till our re - volt - ing's done. It is

2 - L - 8 - 4 - U! We are____ 2 - L - 8 - 4 - U E - R - E - volt - ing!

When I Grow Up/Naughty

Words & Music by Tim Minchin

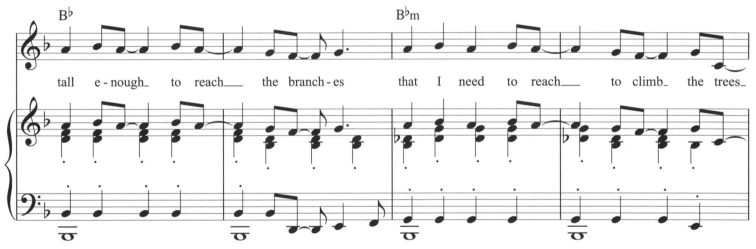

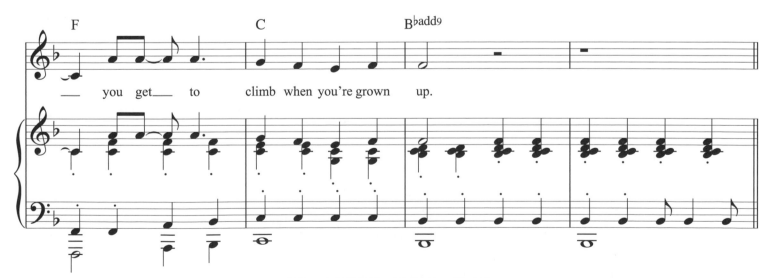

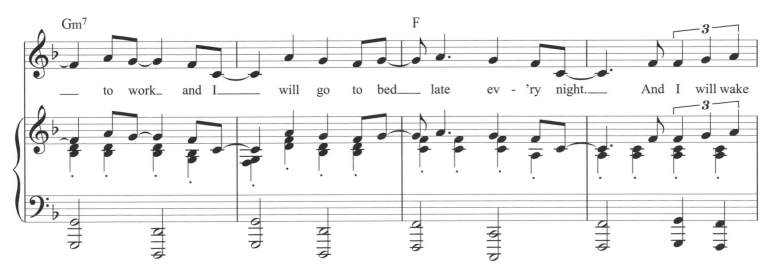

to work___ and I___ will go to bed___ late ev -'ry night.___ And I will wake

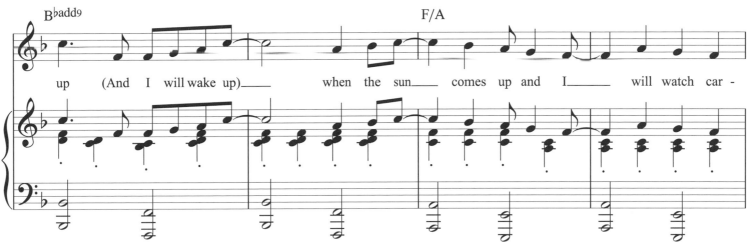

up (And I will wake up)___ when the sun___ comes up and I___ will watch car -

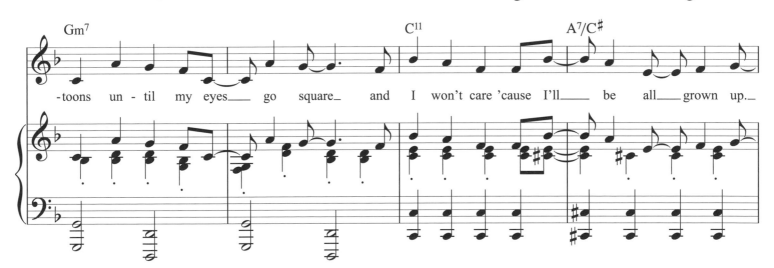

-toons un - til my eyes___ go square___ and I won't care 'cause I'll___ be all___ grown up.___

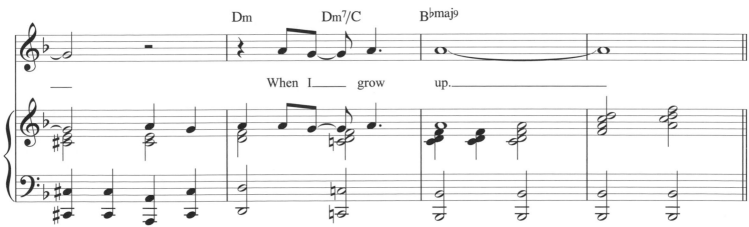

When I___ grow up._____

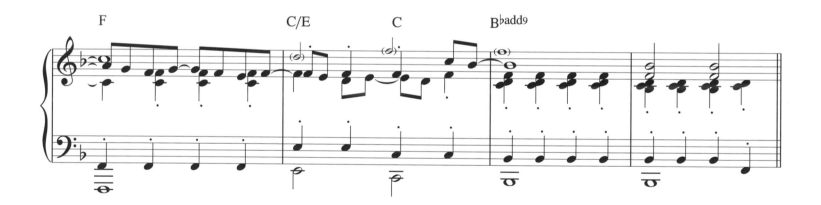

E-ven if you're lit - tle, you can do a lot,___ you must - n't let a lit - tle thing like lit- tle stop_ you.

If you sit a - round and let them get on top,___ you won't change a thing.

Just be - cause you find that life's not fair,___ it___ does - n't mean that you just have to grin and bear___ it. If you al - ways take it on the chin and wear it, you might as well be say - ing you think that it's o - kay. And

that's not right. And if it's___ not right,___

you have to put it right. But no-bod-y else___ is gon-na

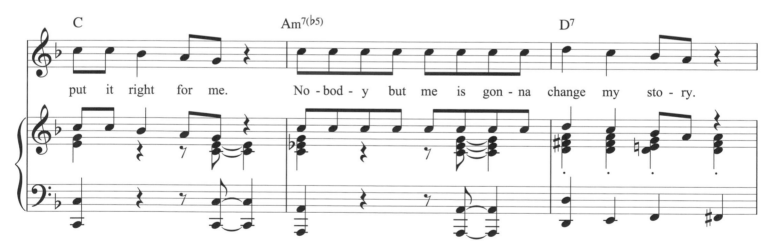

put it right for me. No-bod-y but me is gon-na change my sto-ry.

(TRUNCHBULL:)

Some-times you have to be a lit-tle bit (Mag - gots!) naugh-ty.

142